MW01283125

LICENSE

to

Love

LICENSE

to

Love

DRIVEN BY FAITH

———

Catherine "Kitty" Green

© 2023 by Catherine Green. All rights reserved.

Published by Redemption Press, PO Box 427, Enumclaw, WA 98022. Toll-Free (844) 2REDEEM (273-3336)

Redemption Press is honored to present this title in partnership with the author. The views expressed or implied in this work are those of the author. Redemption Press provides our imprint seal representing design excellence, creative content, and high-quality production.

The author has tried to recreate events, locales, and conversations from memories of them. In order to maintain their anonymity, in some instances the names of individuals, some identifying characteristics, and some details may have been changed, such as physical properties, occupations, and places of residence. The license plate devotions were supplied by many individuals. They are all used by permission.

Noncommercial interests may reproduce portions of this book without the express written permission of the author, provided the text does not exceed five hundred words. When reproducing text from this book, include the following credit line: "*License to Love: Driven by Faith* by Catherine Green. Used by permission."

Commercial interests: No part of this publication may be reproduced in any form, stored in a retrieval system, or transmitted in any form by any means—electronic, photocopy, recording, or otherwise—without prior written permission of the publisher/author, except as provided by United States of America copyright law.

Unless otherwise indicated, all Scripture quotations are from the Holy Bible, New International Version®, NIV®. Copyright © 1973, 1978, 1984, 2011 by Biblica, Inc.™ Used by permission of Zondervan. All rights reserved worldwide. www. zondervan.com. The "NIV" and "New International Version" are trademarks registered in the United States Patent and Trademark Office by Biblica, Inc.™

Scripture quotations marked (esv) are from the esv® Bible (The Holy Bible, English Standard Version®), copyright © 2001 by Crossway, a publishing ministry of Good News Publishers. Used by permission. All rights reserved. The esv text may not be quoted in any publication made available to the public by a Creative Commons license. The esv may not be translated in whole or in part into any other language.

Scripture quotations marked (kjv) are taken from the King James Version, public domain.

Scripture quotations marked (The Message) are taken from The Message, copyright © 1993, 2002, 2018 by Eugene H. Peterson. Used by permission of NavPress. All rights reserved. Represented by Tyndale House Publishers.

Scripture quotations marked (nlt) are taken from the Holy Bible, New Living Translation, copyright ©1996, 2004, 2015 by Tyndale House Foundation. Used by permission of Tyndale House Publishers, Carol Stream, Illinois 60188. All rights reserved.

Scripture quotations marked (NET) are quoted by permission. Quotations are from the net Bible® copyright ©1996, 2019 by Biblical Studies Press, L.L.C. http://netbible.com. All rights reserved.

The artwork "Answered Prayer" was used by permission by artist Dave McCamon (Davemccamon@yahoo.com).

ISBN 13: 978-1-64645-359-7 (Paperback)
978-1-64645-358-0 (ePub)
Library of Congress Catalog Card Number: 2023909984

CONTENTS

DEDICATION

Thank you!

Thank you for allowing me to write this book. It chronicles my journey through losing my brother, Jerome "Jerry" Hayes, and the support that I received from my family and friends.

I dedicate this book to my beloved brother. Thank you, Jerry. Thank you for the memories we shared and for your children, Annemarie, Rosemary, and Jack. You might be gone but never forgotten.

I'd also like to thank my husband, Don, our daughters, Katie and Jackie, and my siblings, Michael and Maureen (Mo). Thank you for being that beacon of hope to keep Jerry's memory alive.

Dear family and friends,

Thank you for joining me through all these years of seeing Christian license plates. It started as a way for me to make it through the day; to get a sign that everything was going to be okay. As a result, we've shared more than 950 license plates together and the stories they hold for each of us. This became therapeutic as I gathered everyone's stories. I'm grateful to my friends who stuck with me, and together we helped each other.

Love,

Catherine

INTRODUCTION

GOD SPEAKS TO EACH OF us in varying ways as we travel on our life's journey to remind us of His love and presence. For me, God has used ordinary, common license plates to speak words of comfort and strength. Yes, that's right—license plates. In fact, God has used more than 950 license plates to speak to me and numerous others over several years.

Once I started seeing this pattern, I began recording when and where I saw particular plates. My friends and family joined in and began to share their own stories. And before I knew it, we had so many stories to share I wanted to compile some of them into this book.

This all started during one of the saddest times in my life. I lost my dear brother Jerome (known as Jerry or Jer) when he committed suicide. My world was shaken. Jerry was the kindest brother, father, husband, and friend. I fell into a deep depression, not knowing how to face this world without Jerry's bright light. In the midst of that grief, God gave me a license plate to remind me of His love in the midst of my pain. You'll read that story later, but seeing that particular license plate was a profound moment in my life.

Other license plates have reminded me of God's presence, power, and faithfulness. I have seen plates encouraging me to praise God, to sing and to remember that I am blessed. Many of these messages have been received at exactly the moment I or my friends needed them. If I had seen one or two messages of comfort or hope I would be grateful, but for us to have seen more than 950 of them is undeniable.

A year after seeing that first license plate, I was riding in the car with a friend. I told her about the plate, and she was one of the first people to verbally recognize God's role in what I was seeing. I pondered what she said and knew it was true. Over the course of several years, I came to almost expect God to speak to me in this way. I even began praying for friends in need, that God would show them the same simple yet meaningful messages I was being shown.

Many of the stories you will read giving context to the plates seen are written by my friends and acquaintances. At the end of this book, you'll find a list of those credits. Because of the connection we have made by sharing our sightings and stories, God has touched many more lives than my own. For that, I am blessed.

The cars traveling by me on the roads and highways have become analogies for how I see God. Sometimes my life is great, as if driving on a clear and smooth path. At other times, as I face challenges and temptations, I have to navigate pot holes and detours and uphill climbs.

Throughout every journey, God is present, giving me guidance and reminding me of His love for me. I take great comfort in reading Scripture, as well as books by inspirational authors. Squire Rushnell, author of the Godwink series, writes about those times when God shows up and subtly makes His presence known, giving us a *Godwink*. I own all of his books, and I daily follow his wife, Louise Ann Duart, on her Facebook page, "Godwinkers."

Each and every one of the 950 license plates that I or my friends have seen have been reminders of God's presence. They have been *Godwinks*.

I hope you enjoy the short stories written here. More importantly, I hope you reflect on ways God speaks to you and come to realize that God can use any tool at His disposal to make His message known, even if that tool is found on a twelve-inch-by-six-inch metal plate attached to a passing car.

Jesus Image Framed (Jesus image for sale for $28 at a shop). I was at a friend's shop and found this picture of Jesus for $28. I texted my dear friend to ask if I should buy it, but there was no answer. I feel as I was taking pictures of this image of Jesus, which I had never seen before, my brother was taking his life. The owner of the picture gifted it to me. Above the picture was stenciled in gold:
WISH IT, DREAM IT, DO IT!

Jerry in his thirties. I've read so many books, and articles about people dying and going to heaven and back. Near-death experiences. So many say that the old people are no longer old but look to be in their thirties, or even thirty-three, the age Jesus was when he died. In the book Heaven Is for Real the young boy said his grandpa Pops did not look like the picture his dad showed him when he was older. But when his dad showed him a picture of Pops in his thirties, the boy recognized him.

The man in Jesus's embrace resembles my brother Jerry with Jesus. The first time I saw this image, I cried and cried because I already knew Jerry was in Jesus's embrace and in heaven (but this confirmed it to me). The mom of one of Jerry's best friends, Joanne Bunyak, sent me a song titled "One Pair of Hands" by Carroll Roberson. Some think it is Elvis. In the YouTube video, there is the image of a man in Jesus's embrace. I stopped it and played it over and over. Jerry was almost forty-eight when he died, and the image was of him in his thirties.

I've seen this image many times in videos and devotionals. It's the same picture that Lori found. I bought the picture from the artist and he printed the "Journey's End" poem on it. I see this picture every single day, and it brings me peace.

Journey's End
by Derek Hegsted

The storm you weathered,
faithfully stood.
I was beside you
all the way
whisp'ring, you could!

Well done my faithful servant,
for me, you defended.
You stayed your course
your journey has ended.

This is a picture of Jerry and his daughter Rosemary.
"My Father's Love," dated September 30, 2013, by Rhonda Bell.

This devotional came up in my email on a Monday morning. The devotional included a picture of a little girl and man that reminded me of Jerry's youngest, Rosemary, and the man looked like my brother Jerry. Rosemary was on the Homecoming Court that weekend, and I felt like Jerry knew; he was viewing it from heaven, in my opinion. I may be wrong, but I have had the feeling that people in heaven get glimpses of earth.

SECTION 1

COMFORT

LV JESUS / JESUS LV

. . . and from Jesus Christ, who is the faithful witness,
the firstborn from the dead, and the ruler of the
kings of the earth. To him who loves us and has
freed us from our sins by his blood.

REVELATION 1:5

O N THE WAY TO MY brother's funeral, I glanced out the window and saw the license plate LV JESUS (Love Jesus). Just days before, my brother had met Jesus face-to-face. Seeing this license plate brought me comfort at such a tragic time in my life.

A month after the funeral, my friend Joanne sent me a video of the song "One Pair of Hands" by the singer with a voice like Elvis's named Carroll Roberson. In the video, there was an image of a man in the embrace of Jesus. The man resembled my brother Jerry.

I found the artist of the picture, Derek Hegsted, and hoped to get a copy of that picture. My dearest friend, Lori, actually found it at the Salvation Army with the "Journey's End" poem included, and she bought it for me. Sadly, the picture was lost, and she was never able to give it to me. Years later, however, the artist himself sent me the signed picture with the poem.

After Jerry's funeral, I had checked to see if the license plates, LV JESUS or JESUS LV, were available, but they were not. But when my husband bought me a new vehicle, he asked if I wanted to change my M H JESUS (Miracles Happen with Jesus) to another plate. I declined, but a few days later, I decided to recheck both those plates.

JESUS LV was available, so I took it. My new plates remind me of how things come back full circle, like Romans 8:28, and I was meant to change my license plate. LV JESUS (Love Jesus) was the plate I saw after Jerry's death, and JESUS LV (Jesus Love) is the plate I now have on my car. Yes, my dear ones, Jesus loves us, this we know.

Framed Jesus, and Jerry with flashlight from Lori's cell phone camera. Lori was at the Salvation Army with her mom. She texted me to tell me she found something, and she sent me a picture of the actual framed picture by artist Derek Hegsted, "Journey's End," with the poem on the picture. I texted her back and asked if she could take another picture, due to the camera glare. She put the picture in the car's back seat, and later when I asked her to send me the new picture, the picture was gone. It had just disappeared.

Lori was at the Salvation Army with her mom. She texted me to tell me she found something, and she sent me a picture of the actual framed picture by artist Derek Hegsted, Journey's End with the poem on the picture. I texted her back and asked if she could take another picture, due to the camera glare. She put the picture in the car's back seat, and later when I asked her to send me the new picture, the picture was gone. It had just disappeared.

Song: "Jesus Loves Me" by Anna B. Warner

Action Step: Has God ever used something as simple as a license plate to remind you of His love for you? Write about that. Today, be looking for ways He is trying to speak to you.

_____

_____

_____

_____

_____

PRAYER

Jesus, we give thanks to You for loving us with unconditional love. Words cannot express how much that means to us all. You never give up on us and continue to pursue us.
Amen

LOVE JER

. . . and to godliness, mutual affection;
and to mutual affection, love.

2 Peter 1:7

SOME ADULT SIBLING GROUPS CAN be closer than others, and in our family of two brothers and two sisters, we had remained tight-knit. We all had our own families, but we remained in contact, spending holidays together well after our parents had passed. In our group you could say one brother was the "favorite," and that was Jerry. Jerry was the thirdborn, so he was my baby brother, but with his caring and protective nature, he was a leader in terms of who we would turn to for a listening ear and a warm heart. His sudden passing shook our group to the core, leaving us shattered.

My own health suffered after his passing. I had lost not only my brother, but my trusted confidant and friend. We relied on each other, and now he was gone. As I fought through my health issues, Jerry was on my mind and in my prayers constantly. It was in my grief that I began to notice personalized license plates. Friends would also see them and send them with messages pertinent to me. I saw them as *Godwinks* during a time when I needed encouragement. So when my sister called to tell me of the license plate that was before her in our home state, we could barely contain our joy at the message: LOVE JER.

We love you, too, Jerry.

Song: "To Know Him Is to Love Him" by the Teddy Bears

Action Step: Have you suffered a loss in your life of someone you deeply loved? Ask God for a *Godwink* today, a reminder that He not only loves you, but He knows your grief and cares for you.

_____

_____

_____

_____

_____

PRAYER

Heavenly Father, we thank You for all the love and loving-kindness You show to Your people. We are forever grateful, and we love You too.
Amen

CEU N HVN
(SEE YOU IN HEAVEN)

Jesus answered him, "Truly I tell you,
today you will be with me in paradise."

Luke 23:43

TODAY I PRAYED AND ASKED God to show me a sign that my dear friend, William (Bill) Witek, was in heaven. We talked about heaven a lot and about our faith. I just wanted to know he was with Jesus. Within a short period of time, under a half hour, I received a text from a close friend about the license plate her husband saw when his sister passed away: CYA N HVN.

This day she saw CEU N HVN (See You In Heaven) on a license plate, and my heart felt healed.

God often gives me moments like this to let me know He is with me. Shortly after that text about the license plate, a package arrived. It was a framed picture by the artist Derek Hegsted. In it is an image of a man, who resembles my brother Jerry, in Jesus's embrace in heaven, titled "Journey's End." At the same time, "You Mean the World to

Me" necklaces appeared in the mail from Shelley at Sweet Romance Jewelry, both reminding me of my brother Jerry.

Not only did God speak to me through a license plate that day, but He also encouraged me with the arrival of a framed picture and necklaces to remind me of my brother Jerry, who is also in heaven. I am grateful for these God moments. And Bill and Jerry, I can't wait to CEU N HVN.

> "Men of Galilee," they said, "why do you stand here looking into the sky? This same Jesus, who has been taken from you into heaven, will come back in the same way you have seen him go into heaven." (Acts 1:11)

Song: "See You in Heaven" by Hans Christian Jochimsen

Action Step: What can you boldly ask God for today? Be patient with His timing, and let go of expectations for *how* He might choose to answer you. Record your prayer here.

_____

_____

_____

_____

_____

PRAYER

Jesus, You have shown me miraculous miracles here on this earth. You have let me know when my loved ones are with You in heaven. I cannot express what that has meant to me—peace of heart and mind and spirit.

Amen

LVD BY HM

*May our Lord Jesus Christ himself and God our
Father, who loved us and by his grace gave us eternal
encouragement and good hope.*

2 Thessalonians 2:16

ONE DAY, I WAS MISSING my dearest friend, Sue, who had recently passed away. I was talking to God, ready to cry, wondering why I was not seeing any new license plates. My friends and I had seen over nine hundred Christian and positive licenses plates to date.

I was leaving the gym, and one of my doctors told me she saw LVD BY HM (Loved by Him). This was just what I needed at the exact moment. God knew I needed the reassurance. Sue was being loved by Him, Jesus. So many of us have a lot of faith, but we start to crumble when we feel lonely, sad, or at a loss for a loved one, like I felt that day. Praise the Father, Son, and Holy Spirit for this God blessing. We just need to A.S.K. (ask, seek, knock).

Song: "I Am Loved by Him" by Walk of Grace Chapel

Action Step: Can you relate to the feelings of loneliness or sadness when you are missing a loved one? Think about the people in your life today who might also be feeling lonely or sad. How can you be the blessing they need today?

_____

_____

_____

_____

_____

PRAYER

Lord Jesus, thank You for always letting me know how much I am loved by You.
Amen

1 HPY FSH
(ONE HAPPY FISH)

"Come, follow me," Jesus said,
"and I will send you out to fish for people."

Matthew 4:19

I HAD MY FIRST BOUT OF depression and anxiety at forty years old. God kept putting cars in front of me with Christian fish emblems of various kinds. I saw many of them at the zoo where the licenses were from all different states.

I would be struggling with anxiety, and within a few minutes, I would see a fish, and I would thank the Lord. The moment I saw the license plate, 1 HPY FISH (One Happy Fish), and the Christian fish emblem, I immediately thought of Jesus. Three times in my adult life, I have suffered from anxiety and some depression. God and Jesus always pull me through, but I struggle with God's timing to get me well.

IXOYE is a Greek acronym standing for "Jesus Christ, Son of God, Savior." This Greek word is pronounced, ICHTHUS, meaning "fish." Jesus was a fisher of men, and He taught His disciples to also be fishers of men.

This license plate encouraged me to be the "fisher of men" that, as His disciple, He has called me to be. As the Holy Spirit prompts me, I talk with and pray for people, telling them about Jesus's love for them.

Song: "Pray for the Fish" by Randy Travis

Action Step: Has the Holy Spirit ever prompted you to talk with and pray for or with another person? Pray for the Holy Spirit's prompting to be a "fisher of men," asking God to lead you to those who need a word from Him.

_____

_____

_____

_____

_____

PRAYER

Lord Jesus, You found Your disciples and taught them how to fish for men. Please teach us to do the same.
Amen

JER 1

In a moment, in the twinkling of an eye, at the last trumpet. For the trumpet will sound, and the dead will be raised imperishable, and we shall be changed.

1 Corinthians 15:52 ESV

THE LICENSE PLATE, JER 1, is one I have seen more than once, and each time I see it, it reminds me of my younger brother Jerome. I called him Jerry or Jer. In one moment, my younger brother took his life, and eleven years later, I continue to pray for those who loved my brother and are still dealing with his loss.

I know we will all see Jerry again in heaven, but for those of us left behind, it still hurts so much. God and Jesus help me with missing my brother on the many days I feel like I cannot go on without Jerry. Every time I return home from seeing my family and relatives in my hometown, I cry. Grief is an ongoing process and so very different for everyone.

Listening to music helps me in my grief—Christian, oldies from the seventies and eighties. Even though I still struggle with Jerry's loss, it is getting easier. Sounds, scents, music, and places can bring me right back into moments with Jerry and bring me comfort.

But my ultimate comfort is God's constant presence with me.

Song: "Not For a Moment (After All)" by Meredith Andrews

Action Step: Is there a song, a smell, or a place that reminds you of a special moment with a loved one? Write about it.

_____

_____

_____

_____

_____

PRAYER

Heavenly Father, we know so many of our loved ones
have been in Jesus's sweet embrace.
I cannot wait until it is my time to meet Jesus face-to-face
and to experience His loving embrace.
Amen

BELIEVE

For God so loved the world, that he gave his only begotten Son, that whosoever believeth in him should not perish, but have everlasting life.

John 3:16 KJV

*I*T HAS BEEN SAID THAT three times is a charm. That is exactly how I felt that day when I saw three BELIEVE license plates. At times we might feel doubtful because we do not think God hears our prayers. Our prayers are not being answered promptly enough for us. But He wants the best for us, so His timing is always perfect.

To believe without seeing or touching is a hard thing to do. In our world, we need to see something with our own eyes to believe it.

We can only imagine how excited the disciples were when they witnessed Jesus appearing to them after dying on the cross and rising from the dead. Although, poor Thomas, he was left out and did not get to see Jesus. Thomas doubted because he did not see. Jesus appeared to Thomas eight days later. After touching Jesus where His marks were and seeing Him, Thomas believed. Jesus reminds us in John 20:29, "Blessed are those who have not seen and yet have believed."

Sometimes we may feel God is not with us or has abandoned us. God only wants the best for us. He is always near. In Deuteronomy 31:8, it is the Lord that goes before us. He will be with us; He will not leave us nor forsake us. We are not to fear or be dismayed.

Give it a try; believe in God. God is waiting on you. He loves you! Watch and see the beautiful things He will do for you.

Song: "We Believe" by Lauren Daigle

Action Step: What is the hardest thing about believing?

_____

_____

_____

_____

_____

PRAYER

O Lord, because of what is written, we believe that Jesus is the Messiah, the Son of God. And because we believe, we have life in His Name. Thank You, Jesus!
Amen

PSLM 23 4

*Even though I walk through the darkest valley, I will
fear no evil, for you are with me; your rod and your
staff, they comfort me.*

Psalm 23:4

I SAW THIS VERSE ON A license plate after coming home from
my hometown. My mother-in-law had just passed peacefully,
surrounded by her family. She wanted to go to heaven, or home.
Before she passed, she wondered why she had to go through all of this
when she had lived a good life. She questioned why she was suffering,
but she never complained.

That day on the way home after her passing, God spoke through
that license plate, reminding me not to fear and that He was with me.
Lord, thank You for Your loving reminder!

Psalm 23 was extra special because it is one of my favorite
passages. He knows I have been struggling with the loss of my brother
and with health issues. But God is good, and He is teaching me that
no matter what I go through, He is always with me, comforting me.

Songs: "The Lord Is My Shepherd (Twenty-Third Psalm)" by Keith Green and "Psalm 23" by Don Moen

Action Step: A shepherd's rod and staff help keep the sheep safe from wild animals and from wandering off away from the herd. The Lord's rod and staff can do the same for us. We can be comforted knowing He is protecting us and keeping us close, even when it may not feel like it. What is one area of your life you need to be comforted in today?

_____

_____

_____

_____

_____

PRAYER

We thank You, Father, that even though we walk through the valley of the shadow of death, we have nothing to fear because You are with us.
Amen

1 MOMENT

It will happen in a moment, in the blink of an eye,
when the last trumpet is blown.
For when the trumpet sounds, those who have died
will be raised to live forever.
And we who are living will also be transformed.

1 Corinthians 15:52 NLT

SEEING THIS MADE ME THINK of my brother Jerry, and how in one moment in time, everything can change. It did for all of us, his family of origin, his nuclear family, his loved ones. Everyone who knew my brother loved him. He was the kindest, most loving, hilarious husband, father, brother, and friend.

When we were children, he would get up early to walk me to school, even though his school started later than mine.

In one moment, Jerry was gone from this life, but his many moments of love for others are alive in all of our memories. In a moment, all of us will move from this life to the next. In a moment, those of us in Christ will be raised from death to eternal life. Are we ready?

Songs: "One Moment in Time" by Whitney Houston and "Keep Me in the Moment" by Jeremy Camp

Action Step: How can you live each moment here with eternity in mind?

_____

_____

<u>PRAYER</u>

Lord, in one moment You can change everything
and make all things new! May we look forward to the
MOMENT we see You face-to-face,
thanking You for Your amazing grace.
Amen

2 GOD B

But thanks be to God! He gives us the victory
through our Lord Jesus Christ.

1 Corinthians 15:57

WHEN I FIRST SAW 2 GOD B, I thought of the verse that says, "To [God] be glory" (Galatians 1:5), but then I remembered the song by Fanny Crosby "To God Be the Glory,"

To God be the glory, great things he has done!
So loved he the world that he gave us his Son,
who yielded his life an atonement for sin,
and opened the life-gate that all may go in.

Some people have come and gone in my life. Until we meet again, I think of my family in heaven, and I wonder what they are doing there. Also until we meet again, I think when my visiting family and friends come and go, I will miss them so. Loving and losing people can be extremely hard.

God has been so good to me. He brings things to my mind just when I need them. He brings people into my life just when I need them. Until we meet again at the feet of Jesus, I pray that God will be with each one of them.

Song: "God Be with You" by Selah

Action Step: Take a moment and make a list of those you look forward to seeing in heaven. Thank God for how they have blessed your life.

_____

_____

_____

_____

_____

PRAYER

God, to God be the glory. We love You and are blessed by all the love You have for each of us; we are fearfully and wonderfully made.
Amen

BAGPIPR

They sing to the tambourine and the lyre
and rejoice to the sound of the pipe.

Job 21:12 ESV

*I*T HAD BEEN A VERY difficult and heart-wrenching four months that marked the end of Mom's last days on earth. Through the pain, we were ready to celebrate the great wonder of her loving life as we prepared our tributes to her—tributes to be shared with those whose lives she had touched in her much-too-short eighty-six years.

Once you met Mary Ellen, it did not take very long for you to realize that her faith, family, and friends gave meaning to her life. You also quickly realized that she had an unquenchable love for the University of Dayton—especially the basketball team.

Only stronger than her love of the UD team was her unmistakable pride in her Irish heritage. It was this love of Ireland that led my husband to say, the day before her funeral, that we should have a bagpiper in her honor. Why hadn't I thought of this Irish tribute? The decision was easy. The execution of it was another story.

After hours of fruitless phone calls, I thanked my husband for his hard work and gave him "permission" to walk away. I thanked him for his great efforts to make this Irish moment happen.

An hour later, my husband left the house to pick up food trays for the funeral. Within five minutes of our house, he noticed that the car in front of him bore the license plate that read, "BAGPIPR." I am sure the poor gentleman who was driving the car must have felt a little nervous as he became aware of the wild honking coming from the car behind him. My husband was eventually able to pass him and, with a desperate wave, persuaded him to pull over.

After quickly explaining his frantic efforts to get this "formal" meeting, my husband introduced himself and his purpose. Yes, the man assured him, he was indeed a bagpiper.

It snowed that December morning. The air was cold and crisp as we left the parish church, having just celebrated a beautiful concelebrated Memorial Mass for Mom. As family and friends processed those last steps with Mom to her earthly resting place, next to her beloved of fifty years, "Jack," we all rejoiced in the classic, almost heavenly, clear notes of "Danny Boy." The bagpiper was there to welcome her home.

Song: "Danny Boy" by Celtic Woman

Action Step: Is there a song or an instrument that reminds you of a moment in the past or a loved one? How can God use that moment to encourage you today?

_____

_____

_____

PRAYER

Lord, thank You for the gift of music, which is throughout the entire Bible. So many gifted people have been blessed by Your Holy Spirit teaching them hymns, music, lyrics.
Amen

B JOYOUS

*Count it all joy, my brothers, when you meet trials of
various kinds, for you know that the testing of your
faith produces steadfastness. And let steadfastness
have its full effect, that you may be perfect and
complete, lacking in nothing.*

James 1:2-4 ESV

I WAS LEAVING A FUNERAL. IT had been a sudden, accidental death.
As I was heading out, I wondered to myself, *How can the family
and loved ones B JOYOUS?*

In James 1:2–4, we see that it is our trials that strengthen us and
make us more like Christ. They are painful, and when a loved one
dies, we feel great sadness and suffering. As Christians, Jesus shows
us that it's *through* our suffering that we experience joy: "Looking to
Jesus, the founder and perfecter of our faith, who for the joy that was
set before him endured the cross . . ." (Hebrews 12:2 ESV).

There is something deeply spiritual about the work of suffering
that produces joy in us. To the world, this is foolishness. Suffering
should be avoided at all costs. But we serve a God with an upside-

down kingdom who tells us that it is through our trials that we will grow closer to Him, which produces great joy.

Attending a funeral will always bring grief, but we serve a God who fills us with His joy and His Spirit, emboldening us to continue our journey home.

Song: "The Greatest" by Coko

Action Step: How can you pursue joy in the middle of a current trial?

_____

_____

_____

_____

_____

PRAYER

Dear God, help me to be joyous in all things.
Joy is in the Bible 242 times.
Amen

MS U JOSH

But the mercy of the LORD is from everlasting to
everlasting upon them that fear him, and his
righteousness unto children's children.

Psalm 103:17 KJV

*I*CHOSE THIS LICENSE PLATE TO honor the short life of my son, Joshua Link Dooley, who left this world by suicide on September 15, 1993, when he was sixteen years old. There was no time for goodbyes, and the survivors were left with so much guilt.

I always told people I could survive anything except the death of a child. I started on this journey of grief with my Lord Jesus carrying me, and I discovered that with God's help, I was able to live after the sudden loss of my precious firstborn.

I now have a ministry to help people who are walking through the death of a loved one.

This is a much-needed ministry, one that most churches are not equipped to handle.

The Lord has given me a definite word that Joshua is with Him and in His care, and I will continue my ministry until I am reunited with Joshua in heaven. In the meantime, this license plate has opened up many doors for conversations with complete strangers to share about my son's life and the love of my precious Savior.

Song: "Joshua Fit the Battle of Jericho" by Mahalia Jackson

Action Step: God uses our grief and pain to comfort others. How has God used an experience of yours to comfort others?

_____

_____

_____

_____

_____

PRAYER

Jesus, You know that a lot of us miss our loved ones who are in heaven with You and God. Help us when our hearts are troubled. Give us peace in our hearts and minds.
Amen

PRAZ GOD

*Praise the L*ORD*. Praise God in his sanctuary;*
praise him in his mighty heavens.
Praise him for his acts of power;
praise him for his surpassing greatness.
Praise him with the sounding of the trumpet,
praise him with the harp and lyre.

Psalm 150:1-3

*P*RAZ GOD IS A CALL to prayer, worship and a relationship with God. The plate means, "Praise Him." God and our Lord Jesus Christ want our praises. God has His eyes moving to and fro looking for people He can use; He wants to use us all.

"Here I Am. Send Me!" (Isaiah 6:8) is what I say to my heavenly Father. I will always praise Him, even in the worst of times, during losses, trials, tribulations, valleys, storms, and whatever else can be a hurt to us.

In our darkest times, it is when we praise the Lord that we find our peace and our strength. Through our worship on our darkest days, we can experience the joy of the Lord.

Song: "May the Peoples Praise You" by Keith Getty

Action Step: Take a few minutes and write down several specific things, people, or experiences for which you are grateful to God.

_____

_____

_____

_____

_____

PRAYER

You, O God, are most worthy of our praise. We praise You with our hearts and songs. We praise You for Your faithfulness and for Your great power and love.

Amen

PRAZHIM

He is the one you praise; he is your God,
who performed for you those great
and awesome wonders you saw
with your own eyes.

Deuteronomy 10:21

*I*T CAN BE HARD TO praise God in our storms, trials, and tribulations, but the Bible tells us to do so. As we read in the last chapter, the book of Psalms ends with a chapter all about praising Him and is worth meditating on once again:

Praise the LORD.
Praise God in his sanctuary;
praise him in his mighty heavens.
Praise him for his acts of power;
praise him for his surpassing greatness.
Praise him with the sounding of the trumpet,
praise him with the harp and lyre,
praise him with timbrel and dancing,

praise him with the strings and pipe,
praise him with the clash of cymbals,
praise him with resounding cymbals.
Let everything that has breath praise the LORD.
Praise the LORD.

(Psalm 150)

I have had a difficult time praising God in my situations of life these past nine years. In the past four years, I have struggled with anxiety, but listening to and singing along with worship and praise songs help me praise Him.

Songs: "Praise God From Whom All Blessing Flow" and "Give Praise to Jesus" by Don Moen

Action Step: Take some time today listen to and sing some of your favorite worship songs, or listen to the ones above.

_____

_____

_____

_____

_____

PRAYER

I sing praises to my heavenly Father and my Lord Jesus Christ—the Holy Spirit lives inside of me and helps me, prompting me to praise.

Amen

2 JESUS

I will guide you along the best pathway for your life.
I will advise you and watch over you.

Psalm 32:8 NLT

To Jesus I go, turning to Him, running to Jesus, praying and asking for His help in situations that I cannot handle. Running to Jesus's arms, letting Him hold me, like the young boy who said, "I want a Jesus with skin on Him to hold on to."

How many of us want the very same thing? We know the Holy Spirit is speaking to us, giving us instructions, telling us to help this person or that person; we just want to know that we are hearing from Jesus and the Holy Spirit, that we are responding to Him and not to our own thoughts and desires. In order to hear God's voice, we must abide in Him and stay close to Him by being in His Word, praying, and staying in fellowship with other believers. We were made for community, just like the Trinity, and He speaks to us when we abide in these ways.

Song: "Jesus, I Love Calling Your Name" by Shirley Caesar

Action Step: Read John 15:1–13. Notice how many times the word "abide" or "remain" is used. How does the image of the vine and branches help you better understand the meaning of abiding in Christ?

_____

_____

_____

_____

_____

PRAYER

All to Jesus, we surrender and give ourselves to You. Fill us with Your love and power, and help us humble ourselves to Your glorious Name.
Amen

GOODBYE

Your love, L<small>ORD</small>, reaches to the heavens,
your faithfulness to the skies.

Psalm 36:5

MY BROTHER PASSED AWAY BY suicide, so no goodbyes were shared. A month after Jerry went to be with the Lord, Jesus let me see an image of a man in His embrace. That image was of a picture we had placed in a locket and given to one of his daughters. Even though the wound is many years old, the scar is still there. It is comforting to know we will all be together one day as a family, reunited in heaven.

While I may not have gotten to say goodbye, God's love covers us like the sky covers the earth, and that same love that covers me covers Jerry, keeping us connected while we are apart. My Jerry is absent from the body and present with the Lord, greeted by Jesus. And once we all enter heaven, we will never have to say goodbye again.

*My daughter Katie and I went to make pictures small enough to fit
into the lockets that my sister Maureen (Mo) and I had bought for
Jerry's two daughters, Annemarie and Rosemary. We bought a Saint
Christopher necklace for his son, John Michael (Jack), because we
could not find a cross his size. That picture of Jerry is where it all
started. Later, I would see a man in Jesus's embrace that resembled my
Jerry. Had we not had that picture and put it in Annemarie's locket,
I never would have made any connection.*

My daughter Katie and I went to make pictures small enough
to fit into the lockets that my sister Maureen (Mo) and I had bought
for Jerry's two daughters, Annemarie and Rosemary. We bought a
Saint Christopher necklace for his son, John Michael (Jack), because
we could not find a cross his size. That picture of Jerry is where it all
started. Later, I would see a man in Jesus's embrace that resembled my
Jerry. Had we not had that picture and put it in Annemarie's locket,
I *never* would have made any connection.

Song: "Brother" by NEEDTOBREATHE and Gavin DeGraw

Action Step: Think about an experience where you didn't get to say goodbye. How did it make you feel at the time? What is your perspective now?

_____

_____

_____

_____

_____

PRAYER

Dear Jesus, when You were on the cross, You were only able to say goodbye to Your mother, Mary, and disciple John, and other women. You came back to everyone when the Holy Spirit came. Thank You, Jesus.
Amen

NO FEAR

Peace I leave with you, my peace I give unto you:
not as the world giveth, give I unto you. Let not your
heart be troubled, neither let it be afraid.

John 14:27 KJV

OVER THE PAST SEVERAL YEARS, I have dealt with anxiety, and I have been frightened. But God tell us in Scripture not to be afraid:

> But now, this is what the LORD says—
> he who created you, Jacob,
> he who formed you, Israel:
> "Do not fear, for I have redeemed you;
> I have summoned you by name; you are mine."

(Isaiah 43:1)

> So do not fear, for I am with you;
> do not be dismayed, for I am your God.

I will strengthen you and help you;
I will uphold you with my righteous right hand.

(Isaiah 41:10)

Over the years, I have seen several license plates that remind me not to be afraid:

NO FEAR NO FEER
DNT WRY (DON'T WORRY) DNT WRRY NT2WORRY
DNT PANC DNT PANC (DON'T PANIC)
1 PET 5 7 1PTR5V7 (1 PETER 5 7)
DNT GV UP DT GIV UP (DON'T GIVE UP)
NVA GV UP (NEVER GIVE UP)

So how do we give our fear over to God? In Veronica Petrucci's song "No Fear" she tells us that spending time in Scripture helps us to be unafraid.

When we spend time with God and in His Word, He will instill the courage we need to overcome our fears and anxiety.

Songs: "Through the Storm" by Yolanda Adams and "No Fear" by Veronica Petrucci

Action Step: What is something that currently brings you fear? Memorize Isaiah 41:10 and repeat it every time you feel afraid. Watch as you are strengthened by God!

_____

_____

_____

_____

_____

PRAYER

Father, You tell us not to fear. May we remember when fear creeps in that You say, "'So do not fear, for I am with you; do not be dismayed, for I am your God. I will strengthen you and help you; I will uphold you with my righteous right hand."
Amen

GODLVU & JC LUVS U

Precious in the sight of the LORD
is the death of his faithful servants.

Psalm 116:15

*I*SAW THESE PLATES ON A bike ride on Memorial Day, and they reminded me of those who have blessed me and went on to live with Jesus, especially my grandmother and aunt, who taught me about Jesus. Because of great God's love, I have been loved well by others.

Recently, I had not been seeing many license plates. I was praying to God and Jesus about this, and all of a sudden I saw GODLVU, with the license plate cover saying JESUS inside a fish emblem. I thanked God for His reminder of His love for me and for us all. A week later, my friend sent me the license plate, JC LUVS U (Jesus Christ Loves You). Again, I thanked my friend and Jesus for the perfect timing. I was writing that day and working on the book cover when she sent it to me. It was perfect timing—two holy moments. Words cannot describe how my heart and mind feel when I get these special messages from above. I yearn for the day I see Jesus face-to-face in heaven and can experience His love even more.

Song: "The Blessing" by Hillsong

Action Step: As you go through your day, dwell on His great love for you and seek how He might have you share that love with someone.

_____

_____

_____

_____

_____

PRAYER

Lord, thank You for Your many blessings,
to us Your children, forever grateful.
Amen

I AM HIS

"Isn't this the carpenter?
Isn't this Mary's son and the brother of
James, Joseph, Judas and Simon?
Aren't his sisters here with us?"
And they took offense at him.

Mark 6:3

*I*WAS ON THE PHONE WITH a person who was telling me about a funeral that I had been unable to attend. I was dealing at the time with the worst anxiety I had ever experienced. As she talked about the viewing and funeral, she made hurtful remarks about my mom. I could not believe what I was hearing, and I was shocked by it.

As I got off the phone, I was so upset, anxious, and even depressed. I went downstairs to get my cell phone that was charging, and when I picked it up, there was a text from one of my best friends, Lisa, with a picture.

The picture was a license plate that said: I AM HIS. The license plate frame said, "My Boss Is a Jewish Carpenter." My mom had that saying on a bumper sticker, and two wood plaques in her home had the same saying. She knew she was HIS.

I cried, thanking God for being so personal, so comforting, in the exact time I needed this message. While my friend's remarks were hurtful, God's words to me through this license plate, *I am His,* were healing.

Song: "Jesus Was a Carpenter" by Johnny Cash

Action Step: As you go throughout your day, look for opportunities to speak words of life to someone who needs it, remembering that *you are His.*

_____

_____

_____

_____

_____

PRAYER

Jesus, I am Yours now and forever more.
Amen

JESU5

"Come, follow me," Jesus said,
"and I will send you out to fish for people."

Matthew 4:19

ON MY WAY HOME FROM a doctor's appointment one day, the car in front of me had a license plate which read, "JESU5."

My son was driving because I was still recovering from a broken leg. Our route had just taken us past a rehab center that I had just spent six weeks living at due to my broken leg.

As we passed by, I mentioned to my son how happy I was to be out of there. I was very depressed there, couldn't walk, and just wanted to be home.

I would visit the chapel daily at the rehab center and pray for God to help me and all the other residents there, to get through the recovery period that we were there for. Seeing this license plate reminded me that indeed, my prayer was answered, and Jesus was with me the whole way.

Song: "Jesus" by Chris Tomlin

Action Step: Looking back over your life, can you remember a time when Jesus was there with you when you didn't even realize it until later? How can this encourage you today to know that Jesus is with you and will get you through?

_____

_____

_____

_____

_____

PRAYER

Dear Jesus, I seek You in my darkest moments. Thank You, Jesus, for always being there. Amen

FLE 2 GOD

But you, man of God, flee from all this,
and pursue righteousness, godliness, faith, love,
endurance and gentleness.

1 Timothy 6:11

*I*WAS STRUGGLING WITH INFECTIONS AND anxiety, and I was beyond frustrated and discouraged. I had been crying off and on all day, missing my best friend, Ronda, who lived far away. When I came home from the doctor's appointment, Ronda had sent me the biggest Hello Kitty balloon I had ever seen.

Sometimes God puts people in our paths, using Bible readings, cards, or calls from loved ones to speak to us and remind us of His love for us and that He is ever present in our suffering. That day, He sent Ronda to encourage me.

Jesus tells us in Matthew 11:28 (NLT) to "Come to me, all of you who are weary and carry heavy burdens, and I will give you rest." When we flee to God, run to Him, He meets us there. In my life, He has used license plates over and over to speak to me, and by turning to Him, He gives me rest from my trials. And He wants to give you rest too.

Song: "Flee From Sin/Run To Jesus" by 20schemes Music

Action Step: How can you *flee to God* today?

PRAYER

Dear God, You tell us to come to You, we who are weary, and You will give us rest. We can run to You, flee to You, walk to You, bless You that You are with us always.
Amen

SECTION 2

SALVATION

BELIEVER

*It gave me great joy when some believers came and
testified about your faithfulness to the truth, telling
how you continue to walk in it.*

3 John 1:3

WHEN I BECAME A BELIEVER in Christ, the words from Rhett
Walker's song "Believer" resonated with me.

Are you a believer? When we truly trust in God and His
Word, the Holy Spirit will pursue us to believe in Jesus Christ. Once
we turn, repent, ask God to forgive our sins, and say with our mouths
we believe Jesus is the Lord of our lives, we will be saved.

When I share my story with someone about being born again,
I ask the Holy Spirit to fill me with His wisdom. We do not always
know if something we say will be a stepping stone for someone, but
when we speak openly about God, we can trust Him to use us for
His glory.

After I share my salvation story, I give each person a handmade
bracelet from Bosnia to remind them they are loved by God. When
we become a believer, something truly changes inside and we do
indeed "walk a bit different."

Song: "Believer" by Rhett Walker

Action Step: If you are a believer in Christ, pray about who you can share your salvation story with. To help you feel more confident, take some time to write it out.

_____

_____

_____

_____

_____

PRAYER

Dearest God, thank You for calling me one of Your chosen children. I thank You for helping me believe and turning me into a believer.
Amen

MERCY

The steadfast love of the LORD never ceases;
his mercies never come to an end;
they are new every morning;
great is your faithfulness.

Lamentations 3:22–23 ESV

WHEN I SAW THIS LICENSE plate, MERCY, I thought about the mercy God gives each one of us. A Google search for the definition of mercy reveals, "Compassion or forgiveness shown toward someone who it is within one's power to punish."

Mercy can be used in so many ways. I truly believe we serve a merciful God, and God's mercies are new each morning! God's Word tells us His mercies are never ceasing. How good to know He understands and is merciful. Trust God by talking to Him about everything. Vent to Him. He will answer you in *His* timing, and it will be the best for you, even if you yourself may not agree. Allow *His* mercy to be around you, because when we pray, obey, and wait, His grace and mercy will surely cover us in peace.

God has been so merciful to me and my loved ones. At times we do not see or feel His mercy, but later, looking back we can see where He was with us the entire time.

Song: "Great Is Your Mercy" by Donnie McClurkin

Action Step: How has God been merciful to you?

_____

_____

_____

_____

_____

PRAYER

Lord Jesus, we are thankful for all
Your tender mercies for us.
Amen

01 WAY JC

Jesus answered, "I am the way and the truth and the life. No one comes to the Father except through me."

John 14:6

I HAD BEEN THINKING ABOUT ONE of my best friends, Lisa, and how she shares license plates with me just at the moment I need to see them. I was praying and had a feeling she was going to give me a God message by sending me a license plate. Sure enough, that day I was still thinking about her, and she texted me the plate, 01 WAY JC. We both knew what that meant to us—there is only one way to come to God—through His Son Jesus Christ.

There are times when God reveals Himself to us that we should not ignore. This license plate was a way He revealed Himself to me. He reminded me and my friend that Jesus came so that we may have life in Him and be saved. Our eternal life is secure in Him. My prayer is that others who see this license plate might also receive a God message, a gracious reminder of why He brought Jesus to this earth.

Song: "Who Is the Redeemer of God's Elect?" by Dana Dirksen

Action Step: Scripture tells us that Jesus is the only way to come to God. What does that mean to you?

_____

_____

_____

_____

_____

PRAYER

Lord Jesus, thank you for showing us
the way to You.
Amen

I AM

*God said to Moses, "I AM WHO I AM. This is what you
are to say to the Israelites: 'I AM has sent me to you.'"*

Exodus 3:14

OD IS THE GREAT I AM, and in Exodus, He reveals this name
to Moses. God is ever present with us. He has always existed
and always will. Moses was afraid to go before Pharaoh; God
calmed him by revealing this name, I AM, reminding Moses that He
would be ever present with him.

While God is the great I AM, we also learn in Scripture about
how God sees us. I saw this plaque that reminds me who I am in
Christ:

I am called of God—2 Timothy 1:9
I am chosen—1 Thessalonians 1:4
I am the apple of my Father's eye—Psalm 17:8
I am being changed into His image—2 Corinthians 3:18
I am a new creation—2 Corinthians 5:17
I am the temple of the Holy Spirit—1 Corinthians 6:19
I am forgiven of all my sins—Ephesians 1:7

I am redeemed from the curse of the law—Galatians 3:13
I am blessed—Galatians 3:9
I am above and not beneath—Deuteronomy 28:13
I am elect—Colossians 3:12
I am victorious—Revelation 12:11
I am one in Christ—John 17:21
I am fearfully and wonderfully made—Psalm 139:14
I am set free—John 8:32

Songs: "I Am" by Eddie James and "I Am" by Mark Schultz

Action Step: How does the name of God, I AM, encourage you today? Which one of the "I am" statements above do you struggle to believe?

_____

_____

_____

_____

_____

PRAYER

Loving Father, we know You by many names.
Yet it is only You that is and was and is to come.
Let me know You in all that You are.
Amen

AMZGRC

*May the grace of the Lord Jesus Christ,
and the love of God, and the fellowship of the
Holy Spirit be with you all.*

2 Corinthians 13:14

*I*N THIS DAY AND AGE, the word "wretch" sounds like an unpleasant or terrible word or person. The famous song, "Amazing Grace," says a lot. God's amazing grace, "how sweet the sound, that saved a wretch like me!"

A Google search for the definition of a wretch gives "an unfortunate or unhappy person." Because of God's grace, if we so choose to accept it, we can change unfortunate to fortunate, unhappy to happy. Before I was a Christian, I was confused about all aspects of Christianity. Once I accepted that Christ died for my sins, God opened my eyes and helped me understand. He began to give me answers to my many questions through the Holy Spirit who now lived in me.

The rest of the first stanza of "Amazing Grace" says, "I once was lost, but now I am found, was blind but now I see."

What wonderful words! God loves you and me! Will you let Him be the center of your life and know He loves you? What great confidence you will have.

Song: "Amazing Grace" by Celtic Woman

Action Point: Do you have a story of once being lost but now being found? Consider sharing it with someone today.

_____

_____

_____

_____

_____

PRAYER

Lord, Your grace is amazing. May all who have ever been saved and will be saved experience that moment when we realize all that has been done for us, with tears of joy and thanks to Jesus.
Amen

2 SAV US

He has saved us and called us to a holy life—not
because of anything we have done but because of his
own purpose and grace. This grace was given us in
Christ Jesus before the beginning of time.

2 Timothy 1:9

*T*HROUGH THE HOLY SPIRIT, IT is the Lord who saves us, by drawing us into the relationship with Him. Our heavenly Father, Jesus, and the Holy Spirit all continually try to get our attention, no matter what it takes.

While we should not ignore their promptings, God will continue to love us, and Jesus will be at the door knocking, praying we open the door to His knocking. When you let the Trinity save you, the Holy Spirit will come to live inside you. When this happens, you can tell when you're being prompted to do or say something.

God wants us to obey because He always knows what is best for us. When my friend was having a rough time, she ignored a prompt from God for almost three years. When she finally obeyed this seemingly random request from Him, she was given peace for her ongoing issue. If only she had obeyed sooner!

We might question if what we are hearing or feeling is really from the Holy Spirit, but God will let us know. At times we could miss out on something special, like bringing someone to the Lord or experiencing His peace, if we don't listen to the promptings and act on them.

Song: "Maybe They're On to Us" by NEEDTOBREATHE

Action Step: Have you experienced a time when you felt a conviction in your heart to do something for God? What was your response? The next time you are prompted to act by the Holy Spirit but aren't quite sure about it, talk with a Christian friend or pastor about it.

_____

_____

_____

_____

_____

PRAYER

Jesus, You came to this earth to live with us, suffer for us, die for us, and save us. It's overwhelming to know the love You have for us, and today I pray that You will know the love I have for You.

Amen

WHO AM I

Jesus and his disciples went on to the villages around
Caesarea Philippi. On the way he asked them,
"Who do people say I am?"
They replied, "Some say John the Baptist; others say
Elijah; and still others, one of the prophets."
"But what about you?" he asked. "Who do you say I
am?" Peter answered, "You are the Messiah."

Mark 8:27-30

ESUS ASKED THE DISCIPLE, PETER, "Who do the people say I am?" (Remember God is the great I AM.) Jesus told Peter he would not have known who Jesus was if His Father in heaven had not revealed it to Peter. The same is true for us. The Holy Spirit reveals to us about Jesus and our heavenly Father.

The song by Casting Crowns, "Who Am I," reminds us that all we have is because of what Jesus has done, not our own doing.

Jesus is the great I AM, and it's not about who we are. It's about Him and what He's done for us. He is the Messiah, the Christ, the Holy One of God.

Song: "Who Am I" by Casting Crowns

Action Step: Think of a situation in your life where you have made it about you. How can you take that to God and make it about Him instead?

_____

_____

_____

_____

_____

PRAYER

Just as You asked Peter, "Who do you say I am?" may we proclaim to others that "You are the Christ, the Son of the living God."
Amen

RMNS832

He who did not spare his own Son, but gave him
up for us all—how will he not also, along with him,
graciously give us all things?

Romans 8:32

THIS VERSE FILLS ME WITH awe that God could actually love us so much as to give up His own Son. I do not know of anyone who could love another person enough to be willing to die by crucifixion to save them eternally.

One morning a woman approached me at a stop sign and shared that seeing this verse on my license plate touched her in a time of need, and she was thankful for the encouragement. These words represent the gospel and sanctification (being holy and freed from sin because of what Jesus did for us) in a nutshell. God is a giver and freely gives us salvation, freedom, and all the treasures of heaven with and through Christ Jesus.

These words also remind me that He has done everything for my salvation and will do everything to make me holy and free from my sin. I only have to believe and walk in faith that Jesus Christ is Lord.

There is comfort in knowing that He will never leave me nor forsake me.

Song: "Destiny" by Petra

Action Step: What does this Scripture mean to you?

_____

_____

_____

_____

PRAYER

O Father, You did not spare Your own Son but gave Him up for us all. How can we not trust that You will also, along with Him, give us all things?
Amen

ETERNAL

*Now this is eternal life: that they know you, the only
true God, and Jesus Christ, whom you have sent.*

John 17:3

WHAT DOES GOD SAY ABOUT eternal life?

Jesus states in John 10:27–28 (KJV): "My sheep hear my voice, and I know them, and they follow me: And I give unto them eternal life; and they shall never perish." This refers to the personal, heart-to-heart relationship the Christian has with Jesus.

We have an eternity to be with our Lord, and God, and the Holy Spirit. To be with our loved ones again in heaven. *Forever!* There are so many questions we all have about eternal life and what it will be like.

Eternity means freedom from the troubles of this world. It is having delight in communion with Jesus and being able to worship without ceasing. It is being completely content with our eternal family.

Song: "I Am Blessed" by Eternal

Action Step: When you think of eternity with Christ, what do you think about?

_____

_____

_____

_____

_____

PRAYER

Heavenly Father, bless You for Your gift of eternal life with You. You are a personal God who loves His children, and we, too, love You back. Amen

GODKING

My sheep listen to my voice; I know them,
and they follow me. I give them eternal life,
and they shall never perish;
no one will snatch them out of my hand.

John 10:27-28

*I*WAS SELFISH, GOING THROUGH LIFE thinking everything was great, caught up with what the world had to offer. All the time I was calling myself a Christian and attending church every Sunday.

One day, my sin caught up with me, and all was exposed. I was told and realized that I had to get back to trusting God and doing things His way. I struggled with how to do this and feeling my guilt and shame, wondering if God wanted someone like me.

Shortly after, I was driving around with the intention of looking for license plates with a God theme. I thought there was no way I would find any. Then I saw one, and it caught my eye—GODKING. It shook me. It was an answer to my prayer and confirmed that I was on the right track. God really was seeking me to come back to Him.

To allow Him to be my God. To allow Him to be my King. If God could answer me through a license plate, then I wondered in what other ways He could speak to me.

I used to get frustrated by getting stopped by red lights; now I take the time to look around, and I see license plates with a God theme. If you have a God theme on your license plate, it might be the way in which God is speaking to someone. It was for me.

Song: "When You Spoke My Name" by MercyMe

Action Step: When you find yourself in a situation where you feel impatient and have to wait, take the time to look around and ask God to show you Himself.

_____

_____

_____

_____

_____

PRAYER

Holy Lord, I praise Your holy name.
Thank You for blessing us with Your messages through an
everyday license plate. Only a holy, omnipotent God can be
everywhere at all times. We see Your beauty in nature and
the world. We praise You for sending Your words for us to
discover while driving to all the places we need to be.
Amen

EPHES 2 8

For it is by grace you have been saved, through faith—and this is not from yourselves, it is the gift of God.

Ephesians 2:8

E ARE SAVED BY GRACE, through faith. As the Scripture tells us, it is not from ourselves; it is a gift from God. Our God likes to give good gifts to His children, and He never gives up pursuing us.

Jesus draws us to renew our thought patterns, and we begin to change our behavior by the empowering of the Holy Spirit. Just as we increase our health by eating properly, our spiritual life increases by studying God's Word.

Christian maturity begins with binding our minds to the mind of Jesus so we may be one in thought. God's desire is for our lives to match His desire for us.

Song: "Can Anyone Be Saved by His Own Works?" by Dana Dirksen

Action Step: Do you ever struggle to believe you are saved by faith and not works? Why do you suppose that is? If you don't struggle with that, how could you encourage someone else today that they are saved by grace?

_____

_____

_____

_____

_____

PRAYER

Jesus, I thank You for coming into my heart and life. My prayer to You is that all who seek You shall find truth and learn to walk in faith for all the days of their lives. Amen

PSALM 45

*I will perpetuate your memory through all
generations; therefore the nations will praise you
for ever and ever.*

Psalm 45:17

*A*ROYAL WEDDING! IT MIGHT BE fair to say all weddings are royal. After all, we married our king or queen when we were foreigners to such an arrangement with our spouse. As time went by, we learned more and more about each other's likes and dislikes and formed a pattern to our days and nights, together.

Psalm 45 is about a royal wedding with joy and happiness as its theme. It's a plan rich with meaning and worthy of study in its entirety. Many Bible scholars have explained its content, which speaks of a human kingship and marriage but also of a divine kingship and marriage between the church and Jesus Christ. One day the people of God will be eternally wed to our Lord, and certainly that will be the wedding of all royal weddings!

Song: "Psalm 45 (Fairest of All)" by Shane & Shane

Action Step: Read Psalm 45. Notice how the descriptions of the earthly king also refer to our king Jesus. Write down some descriptions that inspire you.

_____

_____

_____

_____

_____

PRAYER

God, I praise You for all that You are and for all that is to come. Let my prayers be pleasing to You like birdsong is to the morning. Let all nations come to praise Your name.

Amen

2ND BORN

Jesus replied, "Very truly I tell you, no one can see
the kingdom of God unless they are born again."

John 3:3

THIS LICENSE PLATE MAY MAKE a person think of a second child in a family, but I am reminded that we are created by God, and as we grow to an age of accountability where we decide to believe in God, it is called "born again" or a "second birth."

When we accept Christ as God's Son and believe in Him, we are born again into eternal life. In John 3, Jesus is explaining this to the Jewish teacher, Nicodemus, who just can't seem to understand how it's possible to enter his mother's womb and be born again. Jesus explains this second birth is a spiritual birth and not a physical one. That this new eternal life is spiritual, and it only comes from believing Jesus is the Son of God.

Spiritual truths can only be revealed to us as we believe in Jesus. Being born again was as if I gained a new set of eyes, and now I see through the lens of Jesus. My being born again was gradual. Jesus was patient with me, and I learned by being in His Word and asking for wisdom. He will freely give us wisdom and many other things; we just need to trust and ask.

Song: "Caribbean Medley" by Donnie McClurkin

Action Step: Read through the story of Nicodemus and Jesus in John 3:1–22 in a couple of different Bible translations, if possible. If you were explaining to someone what it means to be born again, what would you say?

_____

_____

_____

_____

_____

PRAYER

Lord God, thank You for bringing me to You and for the beginning of a new life. Walking with Christ has changed everything I see and do, and I pray for this new life for every person I come in contact with today.
Amen

The Sinner's Prayer (by Dr. Ray Pritchard)

Lord Jesus, for too long I've kept you out of my life. I know that I am a sinner and that I cannot save myself. No longer will I close the door when I hear you knocking. By faith I gratefully receive your gift of salvation. I am ready to trust you as my Lord and Savior. Thank You, Lord Jesus, for coming to earth. I believe you are the Son of God who died on the cross for my sins and rose from the dead on the third day. Thank you for bearing my sins and giving me the gift of eternal life. I believe your words are true. Come into my heart, Lord Jesus, and be my Savior. Amen.

SECTION 3

PRAYER

4 KERRY

I am reminded of your sincere faith, which first lived
in your grandmother Lois and in your mother Eunice
and, I am persuaded, now lives in you also.

2 Timothy 1:5

*I*SAW A PENCIL ARTIST'S WORK at my doctor's office in August of
2010, two months after my brother Jerry passed away. It was a
drawing of an elderly woman in prayer, and you could see tears
coming down her face as she was praying. The image reminded me
of my Irish grandma O'Sullivan, who prayed for everyone all day and
night, praying the rosary. "Jesus, Mary, and Joseph," she would say
several times a day.

The picture was titled "Answered Prayer," and it showed me a
moment where a woman, like my grandmother, realized God would
never leave her.

When I left my doctor's office, I saw the license plate 4 KERRY.
My grandmother was from County Kerry, Ireland. The number
four made me think of my three siblings and me and our special
relationship with our grandma, who often prayed for us to return to
Ireland one day.

When my sister, Maureen, and I traveled to Ireland after Grandma's passing, we rented a car, and it had a scent that reminded us of Grandma. We took it as her way of telling us she knew we had made it back to Ireland.

"Answered Prayer"
by Dave McCamon, a pencil artist

"Answered Prayer"
by Dave McCamon

Song: "The Kingdom of Kerry" by Kevin Collins

Action Step: Have you ever been reminded of a loved one by a certain smell, song, picture, or experience? Journal about it.

_____

_____

_____

_____

_____

PRAYER

Lord, we bless You for families and our ancestors. Family is important to You, as You show us in both the Old Testament and the New Testament. Thank You for providing people who love us.
Amen

PRAY 724

Rejoice always, pray without ceasing,
give thanks in all circumstances; for this is the will
of God in Christ Jesus for you.

1 Thessalonians 5:16–18 ESV

*I*MOST LIKELY WOULD NOT HAVE noticed this license plate if I had not been stopped due to construction on my way to work. I usually do not feel positive outcomes in traffic jams and delays, but seeing this plate made the wait worth it.

The most obvious meaning to me was a reminder I need to pray "all the time," 24/7 and 7/24. My lack of discipline and focus spent in prayer has much room for improvement.

Recently, I was listening to a sermon that mentioned Joseph Scriven's poem, which was later added to music to create the song "What A Friend We Have In Jesus." My curiosity led me to do some research. The poem's original name was "Pray without Ceasing."

Scriven's life was a touching testimony of faith, kindness, and perseverance. He lived through many challenges and tragedies during his life, and sadly, never realized the significance of his poem and the number of lives it touched. It is now one of the most popular Christian songs 130 years after he passed.

The words of this song are so relevant: "What peace we often forfeit, what needless pain we bear all because we do not carry everything to God in prayer." One of the devotionals I read every morning states, "Pray about everything, leave the outcome to Me."

The reoccurring theme is quite obvious! I wonder how many times I have missed direction from Jesus because I was not paying close enough attention or was too busy to notice a sign or license plate nudging me a few steps further.

Song: "What A Friend We Have In Jesus" by Joseph M. Scriven

Action Step: Do you have a favorite hymn? Write about it here. If not, ask a friend who might have one and have them tell you what it means to them.

_____

_____

_____

_____

_____

<u>PRAYER</u>

O God, we are thankful You are available 24/7 to hear our prayers. May we be as faithful to You as You are to us by praying without ceasing, rejoicing always, and giving thanks in all circumstances.

Amen

GOD ANSR

*Call to me and I will answer you and tell you great
and unsearchable things you do not know.*

Jeremiah 33:3

M**Y FAMILY WAS STRUGGLING IN** a major way in the fall of 2017. I was on the road a lot and feeling torn in many directions. As I drove, I spent the time in silence, praying in my thoughts and sometimes aloud. This time, I was asking God for help in knowing what to do, where to turn.

When I saw this license plate, I let my fear and struggles in that moment go and felt my faith in God guide me. God is the answer! God answers our prayers if we only listen. However He chooses to answer our prayers, He Himself is the ultimate answer when we call out to Him.

Song: "God Answers Prayer" by Vinesong

Action Step: Sometimes in prayer, we have expectations of God to answer our prayers the way *we* want. But sometimes, God Himself is the answer. Today, abide in God's presence and see how your focus on Him shifts your day.

_____

_____

_____

_____

_____

<u>PRAYER</u>

Your Word says that if we ask for what we want in prayer and believe we have received it, it will be ours—which means You are a God who answers and hears our prayers.
Amen

AMEN

Our Father which art in heaven,
Hallowed be thy name.
Thy kingdom come, Thy will be done in earth,
as it is in heaven.
Give us this day our daily bread.
And forgive us our debts, as we forgive our debtors.
And lead us not into temptation,
but deliver us from evil: For thine is the kingdom,
and the power, and the glory, for ever.
Amen.

Matthew 6:9–13 KJV

*I*was praying the Lord's Prayer while driving one day. I do that pretty often, and I pray it before bed as well, also saying my prayer requests to our heavenly Father and asking Jesus to intercede.

When the disciples asked Jesus to be taught how to pray, He taught them *Our Father*. The first thing I thought of when I saw the AMEN license plate was the *Our Father* prayer.

"Amen" is in the Bible a number of times (54). I knew it was about endings, so I looked it up when I returned home. When it is uttered at the end of a prayer or hymn, it means "so be it."

As I pray the Lord's Prayer, I am reminded to say, "Amen, so be it," agreeing with Jesus's words that God's will be done in my life.

Songs: "Let the Church Say Amen" by Andrae Crouch and Marvin Winans and "It Is So" (Reprise) by William McDowell

Action Step: Pray the Lord's Prayer, concluding it with *Amen, so be it*, agreeing with God to do His will in your life.

PRAYER

Father, in all I pray, let my amen be what You see as true and what You find to be in agreement with You, and if it is Your will, then let it be true.

Amen

DO IT AGN

*And now, God, do it again—bring rains to our
drought-stricken lives so those who planted their
crops in despair will shout "Yes!" at the harvest, so
those who went off with heavy hearts will come
home laughing, with armloads of blessing.*

Psalm 126:5-6 The Message

*D*O IT AGN REMINDED ME of the story of a young Billy
Graham visiting the home of John Wesley in England in
1940, where he kneeled on the same carpet where Wesley
had two centuries before as he prayed for England's social and spiritual
renewal. There, Graham prayed for revival too, "Oh Lord, do it again!
Do it again!"

At times I will say to God and Jesus, "I don't want to pray for
that person." And I *really* don't want to pray, "Oh Lord, do it again!
Do it again!"

Through the years since my brother Jerry has been gone, I have
prayed without ceasing, surrendered, prayed for forgiveness, prayed
for those who have hurt me and my loved ones, and even prayed

blessings over them. It's hard to pray for those who hurt you, but God will enable you to pray for them and pray blessings over them.

As I prayed for my enemies one day, I found myself praying, "Please Lord, do it again, do it again." "Then I heard the voice of the Lord saying, 'Whom shall I send? And who will go for us?' And I said, 'Here am I. Send me!'" (Isaiah 6:8).

Dearest God, please use me and my family and loved ones. Bring Jesus believers into my prodigals' lives and work out their salvation and the world's salvation, now and in all future generations. Also please heal those who need all kinds of healings.

Song: "Lord Do It" by James Cleveland

Action Step: Is there an "enemy" in your life, someone who has hurt you that you struggle to pray for? Talk to God about them. Ask Him to help you forgive them and pray blessings over them.

_____

_____

_____

_____

_____

PRAYER

Jesus, You paid the price by dying on the cross for us all.
We give thanks without ceasing,
just like we pray without ceasing.
Amen

TELL GOD

Rejoice always, pray without ceasing, give thanks in all circumstances; for this is the will of God in Christ Jesus for you.

1 Thessalonians 5:16–18 ESV

TELL GOD WHAT YOU ARE feeling, seeing, hearing. He already knows. When we pray and talk to God, He hears us, and His answers are *Yes, No, or Wait.* He knows it is hard to hear *No* or *Wait,* but most times it is for our own good. TELL GOD reminds us to talk to Him, our heavenly Father, opening our hearts and minds to Him. We can tell Him the good, the bad, and the ugly, and He still loves us, and He will always love us.

God is happy when we turn (repent) from our sins and tell Him about what we have done or thought. We should feel blessed that no matter how we were brought up, no matter what kind of parents we had, He is our perfect and loving heavenly Father, and He knows what is best for us.

Song: "If I Tell God" by Kurt Carr

Action Step: What is it you need to tell God today? Maybe you had imperfect earthly parents that made it difficult to open up and share your heart. God knows, and He is waiting to embrace and accept you, just as you are. Tell God what's on your heart today.

_____

_____

_____

_____

_____

PRAYER

God, thank You for letting us come to You and tell You what is on our hearts and minds. I pray that we can have our minds bound with Jesus so we may be one, and then bind our minds with You, God, so You and me and Jesus can be one, along with the Holy Spirit.
Amen

PRA N 4 U 2

*For where two or three gather
in my name, there I am with them.*

Matthew 18:20

*I*WAS PUTTING SOME OF MY books away on the shelves in the basement when I moved a book cover, finding a possible license plate written on a piece of paper. It was tucked inside of Henri Nouwen's book, *Spiritual Direction*, and it appeared as if someone was trying to check the availability of a license plate. PRA N 4 U 2 was all underlined.

Or maybe not. It could have been they were leaving a note for a friend to let them know they were "praying for you too."

For some of us, we have been in trials that have lasted years. We have requested prayers, been put on prayers lists, prayer walls, and candles have been lit, sending up prayers to God.

PRA N 4 U 2 reminds us, "For where two or three gather in my name, there am I with them" (Matthew 18:20).

Song: "Wait for Me" by Rebecca St. James

Action Step: Today encourage someone you are praying for them, and then lift them up to God.

_____

_____

_____

_____

_____

PRAYER

Heavenly Father, when I say "praying for you"
to someone, may I be faithful, trusting You to hear my
prayer and work in the situation and
provide what they need.
Amen

EVEN IF

Even if you have been banished to the most distant
land under the heavens, from there the LORD your
God will gather you and bring you back.

Deuteronomy 30:4

*E*VEN IF YOU HAVE QUESTIONS, concerns, or doubts about life, God, or Jesus, it is okay. Jesus tells us in His Word that He would rather we be hot or cold, but not lukewarm, in our faith. If we are lukewarm, He will spit us out. I have questioned and still question things, and many of us do.

I listen to the Divine Mercy Chaplet when I ride my bike or take our Gracie dog for a short walk. One day as we were walking, I saw this license plate. It reminded that God is still good even if we suffer. Even if He doesn't answer my prayers the way I want, He still answers in a way that is best, even though I may not see it. If even if I've lost my brother to suicide, even if I had problems years ago with anxiety, even if a family member is sick, I still believe He has the power to work in those situations for good, and that I trust Him to do what He will do.

Song: "Even If" by MercyMe

Action Step: What is a time in your life when you prayed for something, but God chose to answer it differently? Were you able to see His goodness in it?

_____

_____

_____

_____

_____

PRAYER

Even if You do not answer my prayer or act in a way I had hoped, help me, O Lord, to trust that You know what is best for me. My hope is in You alone.
Amen

SECTION 4

PROVISION

GODDIDT

*For the word of God is alive and active. Sharper
than any double-edged sword, it penetrates even to
dividing soul and spirit, joints and marrow; it judges
the thoughts and attitudes of the heart.*

Hebrews 4:12

MY HUSBAND AND I HAD a very rough several months. We had experienced many recent losses, changes, and life trauma.

One day, my husband said, "Let's go look for license plates!"

I wasn't very optimistic.

But as we drove through the first parking lot, we saw two plates: GODDIDT and MOR2COM.

A month prior, God had revealed many things about our lives that were difficult, and we wrestled with God. I knew it was ultimately for our good. These plates encouraged us that He was up to something, and He would succeed.

Ephesians 6:12 (KJV): "For we wrestle not against flesh and blood, but against principalities, against powers, against the rulers of the darkness of this world, against spiritual wickedness in high places." While things were difficult and we didn't yet see the clear path, we knew God was working behind the scenes to bring hope and healing.

Song: "God Only Knows" by For King and Country

Action Step: Sometimes God doesn't show us a clear path through our difficult situation. But He does encourage us on the journey. If you are going through a hard season, ask for God's encouragement today, and be on the lookout for what He might do!

_____

_____

_____

_____

_____

PRAYER

God, You did it! You gave us a gift of restoration through Your Son, Jesus Christ, putting us in right standing with You. Thank You, Father, for freedom from sin and death!
Amen

OUR FTHR

Our Father which art in heaven, Hallowed be thy name. Thy kingdom come, Thy will be done in earth, as it is in heaven. Give us this day our daily bread. And forgive us our debts, as we forgive our debtors. And lead us not into temptation, but deliver us from evil: For thine is the kingdom, and the power, and the glory, for ever. Amen.

Matthew 6:9-13 KJV

*I*NEVER HAD A REAL FATHER growing up. He left before I was five, and before then, he traveled. As a child I didn't have any connection with him. My brothers-in-law were my father figures. They were all much older than me, as I was part of my mom's second family.

After my rebellious teen and college years, I chose to become Catholic on my own. I was always drawn to the "Our Father" prayer in mass. I grew to think of God as my real Father and still love to say the "Our Father" when I'm in need of prayer and comfort. The more I learned about my heavenly Father, the more I knew that He was in fact my true Father, and He would be the one to guide me and love me unconditionally.

When I saw this particular license plate, of course it spoke to me personally.

Songs: "The Lord's Prayer" by Michael O'Brien and "Our Father" by Don Moen

Action Step: What characteristics about your earthly father or father figure in your life remind you most of God, your heavenly Father?

_____

_____

_____

_____

_____

PRAYER

Our Father, who art in heaven, hallowed be thy name; thy kingdom come; thy will be done on earth as it is in Heaven. Give us this day our daily bread; and forgive us our trespasses as we forgive those who trespass against us; and lead us not into temptation, but deliver us from evil. For thine is the kingdom, and the power, and the glory for ever and ever. Amen

GOD CHSN

*I have seen and I testify that this is
God's Chosen One.*

John 1:34

OUR JOURNEY BEGAN SEVERAL YEARS ago. It was time for a wonderful Women of Faith convention in Columbus, Ohio. My good friend Mary and I signed up and eagerly awaited the day to head to Columbus, hoping we could find the convention center and the hotel! In the meantime, God had a plan for our lives which was very unusual—we were asked if it would be possible for a lovely woman to stay in our room, as the girls she was traveling with had a full room.

Of course we accepted this stranger into our midst, thinking it would be "one and done," as she would stay with her friends after the convention. I could see that she was troubled about something, but, not knowing her, I didn't pry.

In our room that night, she felt comfortable enough with us to talk more openly about her devastating family loss and grief. We provided shoulders to cry on and ears to listen and love. We became

God's chosen "sisters" that night and have stayed connected ever since. God brings people into our lives at His chosen time to bless and be blessed by.

Song: "Even in The Valley" by God's Chosen

Action Step: As you move through your day, be open to seeing an opportunity where God might choose to use you to encourage someone else, even a stranger.

_____

_____

_____

_____

_____

PRAYER

Father God, thank You for choosing us. You picked us before the beginning of time. You have loved us always from the beginning until we reach heaven—then we will be with You forever and ever.
Amen

DNT WRY

Cast all your anxiety on him
because he cares for you.

1 Peter 5:7

WHEN I FIRST SAW DNT WRY, I was with a loved one I was worried about. They were having serious health issues, and I felt helpless and frustrated that I could not help.

I saw that plate over and over the entire weekend. Jesus blessed me so much with that message. It was as if He were saying, "Kitty, you know I love you and your loved ones. Just believe and trust in Me, and don't worry!"

In my town, I saw a similar plate, DNT WRRY. Jesus kept confirming the same message to me. Often God uses license plates, Scriptures, and songs with similar meanings to speak to me.

One day I was struggling with my health and asking Jesus to show me one of the DNT WRY / DNT WRRY license plates. As I was doing errands, I decided to go a different way, and as I turned my head, I saw NT2WRRY.

Our God is so personal when He answers our prayers. That day He gave me a Godsent.

Are you worried? Cast all your cares, burdens, concerns, depression, anxiety, worries, stress, troubles, and busyness on Him, because He cares for you. You are his personal concern, with deepest affection, and He watches over you very carefully with His loving kindness; He cares about you. Let him have all your worries and cares, for He is always thinking about you and watching over everything that concerns you.

Songs: "Don't You Worry" by Jonathan Butler, "Do Not Worry" by Ellie Holcomb, and "Ain't No Need to Worry" by Ruben Studdard

Action Step: Is there something you are worried about today? Take some time to tell God about it and give Him your worry.

_____

_____

_____

_____

_____

PRAYER

God and Jesus, You tell us hundreds of times in the Old and New Testaments not to worry—fear not; be not afraid. Help us to trust in what You have repeatedly told us. Don't worry!
Amen

VICTORY

But thanks be to God! He gives us the victory
through our Lord Jesus Christ.

1 Corinthians 15:57

WHEN I SEE THE LICENSE plates VICTORY and VICTORY 1, I think of the meaning of victory—an act of defeating an enemy or opponent in a battle, game, or other competition. I also think of geese flying in the shape of a V, helping each other in flight.

We, too, can help each other as we battle the Enemy of our souls. God gives us community to encourage us on this journey and help us persevere when we go through difficult trials. As we lean into each other and to God, we will have victory in our spiritual battle through Christ.

Song: "My Victory" by Passion

Action Step: The next time you see geese in flight, in the shape of a V, let it remind you of the victory we have in Christ, and be encouraged!

_____

_____

_____

_____

_____

PRAYER

*Thanks be to You, O God! You give us victory
through our Lord Jesus Christ.
Amen*

GOD WH ME

The Lord himself goes before you and will be with you; he will never leave you nor forsake you. Do not be afraid; do not be discouraged.

Deuteronomy 31:8

*I*HAVE ALWAYS KNOWN I NEEDED God with me to do much of anything. It was a stretch for me when I was asked to consider leadership in BSF (Bible Study Fellowship). I was humbled and surprised. I didn't consider myself a leader and didn't think I was "good enough" to make all the commitments involved. I prayed about it but could get no clear confirmation if I should or should not accept the leadership position.

Then, one day I saw a license plate: GOD WH ME. I was reminded that God would be with me, and if He led me to it, He would get me through it! I also was reminded of the verse, "God is within her, she will not fall" (Psalm 46:5).

God has, indeed, been with me, and I have been truly blessed by both the women I have led and the fellow leaders who also stepped out in faith. If you are not sure about your calling, pray and step out in faith because God is with you.

Song: "Said He Would Be with Me" by Isaiah D. Thomas

Action Step: Is there a decision you are struggling to make? Ask God for wisdom and to reveal Himself to you as you make this decision.

_____

_____

_____

_____

_____

PRAYER

You are always with me, O God,
and will not leave me or forsake me.
Help me not to fear or be dismayed
but to trust You.
Amen

JESUS

Tie them as symbols on your hands and bind them on your foreheads. Write them on the doorframes of your houses and on your gates.

Deuteronomy 6:8-9

*I*BEGAN A PERSONAL RELATIONSHIP WITH Jesus when Jerry died. I was a believer, born again, soon to be baptized, and Jesus in His loving-kindness drew me closer to Himself. I was baptized a year or so after Jerry's passing.

I started giving out *Jesus I Trust in You* Divine Mercy bracelets in 2016. First, I gifted them to family, friends, and loved ones. Later I started gifting them to strangers. I am still doing this. I plan to keep gifting these bracelets to women and men. When the recipients of the bracelets put them on, they have told me, "I am never going to take it off."

Song: "Jesus Paid It All" by The Newsboys

Action Step: Read Deuteronomy 6:1–9 and 2 Corinthians 2:2–3. God knows we often forget His commands. In the Old Testament,

what did He command them to do so they wouldn't forget His laws?
In the New Testament, where has God written His law?

_____

_____

_____

_____

_____

PRAYER

Jesus, we know we have a friend in You.
You bless us and love us.
Thank You for being a friend.
Amen

JOHN 15 7

If you remain in me and my words remain in you, ask whatever you wish, and it will be done for you.

John 15:7

*O*N MY WAY TO WORK one morning, I was at a traffic light about a block from the hospital. The car in front of me had the license plate JOHN 15 7. I knew it was a verse from the Bible, but I couldn't recall it.

So I took a picture of it and sent it to Kitty.

Later, while looking up the verse, I just cried. I had been praying to God to heal my son Michael from his heroin drug addiction. The past five years had been a painful journey through five different hospital admissions, rehabs for treatment, and five relapses. After Michael's first hospitalization at Talbot Hall, I found Al-Anon, and it truly has been life changing for me and my husband, Rob. I did not realize how sick my thinking and actions were until I joined this program. I have learned so much and found a wonderful support group who truly understood what I was going through because they have all "been there" with their loved ones.

I now have a real relationship with God who has a purpose and plan for me!

I learned the first three steps of the Al-Anon program very well:

1. I cannot.
2. He can.
3. I will let Him!

Thankfully, Michael has been clean for over five years and is doing much better physically, mentally, and emotionally.

It was not an accident seeing that particular license plate near Talbot Hall where Michael went for treatment. Back then, I was scared, sad, and overwhelmed. I just knew that God was with me and was going to see Michael through this difficult time as I abided in God and His words, and His wisdom began to abide in me. He granted my prayer, and it was done for me!

It may not have been in my time or plan but in in His plan and purpose, which is divinely perfect! I trust in Him who gives me strength and hope every day.

I was meant to see that license plate. It was a *Godwink* intended just for me.

Songs: "John 15 Scripture Song" by Jonathan Dixon and "How Is Christ Your Prophet" by Dana Dirksen

Action Step: What does it look like to remain in God's words, according to John 15:7? How can you spend time today abiding with Him and in His Word?

_____

_____

_____

_____

_____

PRAYER

Jesus, may we remain in You so that Your Word remains in us. May we trust that if we remain in You, we may ask whatever You wish and You will do it.
Amen

HE FED 5K

The number of those who ate was about five
thousand men, besides women and children.

Matthew 14:21

THIS LICENSE PLATE MAKES MANY people probably wonder, *Did Jesus really feed five thousand with only a small amount of fish and bread?*

Many of the people who were fed by this Rabbi Jesus would have known from their Hebrew Scriptures that God fed their ancestors with manna from heaven while they traveled in the wilderness. This particular miracle of Jesus's would have confirmed that Jesus was who He said He was, the Son of the God of their ancestors who provided for them in the wilderness. And now, God's Son was providing for them.

If God can provide food for thousands in the wilderness and thousands on a hillside, He can provide for you. It's a matter of belief. Will you believe? Look past your doubts and believe in our mighty God that His Son did do this miracle.

Song: "Jireh" by Elevation Worship

Action Step: If we were sitting on that hillside that day, saw Jesus feed the crowds with a little boy's lunch, and remembered how God cared for your ancestors in the wilderness with manna from heaven, how would you respond? What would you be thinking? And now, knowing this, how does this increase your faith?

_____

_____

_____

_____

_____

PRAYER

Jesus, may we remain in You so that Your Word remains in us. May we trust that if we remain in You, we may ask whatever You wish and You will do it.
Amen

2 ABBA

The Spirit you received does not make you slaves,
so that you live in fear again; rather, the Spirit you
received brought about your adoption to sonship.
And by him we cry, "Abba, Father." The Spirit himself
testifies with our spirit that we are God's children.

Romans 8:15-16

I AM GOD'S DAUGHTER. HE IS a good, good Father who gives His children good gifts freely through Christ Jesus. He meets all my needs according to His riches in glory.

My car was totaled one day when I hit a deer. While I was unharmed, the deer did not survive, and neither did my car. I thanked God for my life and asked Him to provide the car He wanted me to have.

When I received my new car, I wanted to honor God with my license plate number and letters. All I have comes from Him. A car is a need in this day and age, and God blessed me with another vehicle, for which I am grateful. I give God glory and chose to honor Him with my license plate—2 ABBA.

Song: "Abba, I Belong to You" by Tonya Baker

Action Step: The name Abba refers to a close intimate relationship a child has with her daddy. God wants that kind of relationship with us where we can cry out to Him with all our needs and concerns. Spend some time crying out to God today, telling Him your heart's desires.

_____

_____

_____

_____

_____

PRAYER

Abba Father, how sweet it was to learn that the Aramaic word for father was used by Jesus and Paul to address God in a relation of personal intimacy. When we hear the word Abba, when we read it and speak it out loud, it is so personal, like we're talking to our heavenly Father affectionately. Thank You for being our Abba Father.
Amen

COURAGE

But Jesus immediately said to them:
"Take courage! It is I. Don't be afraid."

Matthew 14:27

$\mathcal{P}$EOPLE HAVE TOLD ME I have courage, that I am courageous. At times I feel that way, and other times, I feel so lost and scared. Anxious, nervous.

The dictionary defines courage as: *the ability to do something that frightens one. Strength in the face of pain or grief.*

I had to have courage in the events of Jerry's suicide, during a family member's illness, as well as my own ongoing health issues. In all of these situations, I was terrified, but I cried out to God for His help. I needed God's strength in the face of my deep pain and grief.

When Jesus walked across water to the boat where his disciples were, they were terrified because they thought He was a ghost.

He told them, "Take courage! It is I. Don't be afraid."

Jesus's presence calmed their fears, and He wants to do the same for us. God's presence emboldens us with courage. We can face our fears and have courage when we cry out to Him.

Song: "Take Courage" by Kristene DiMarco

Action Step: Is there a situation in your life that causes fear? Do you need to courage to face it? Write about that experience and ask God to embolden you with His courage today.

_____

_____

_____

_____

_____

PRAYER

Dear God, thank You for giving us courage to get through this life. So many in the biblical times were courageous. Help me to be strong and have the courage to move forward and keep going.

Amen

A WISH 4 U

*The Lord bless you and keep you; the Lord make his
face shine on you and be gracious to you; the Lord turn
his face toward you and give you peace.*

Numbers 6:24-26

*T*HIS LICENSE PLATE REMINDS ME that God has given me countless
material gifts in my life, but more importantly, He has provided
for me spiritually beyond measure.

I am an only child. Growing up, I learned to occupy myself in
creative ways, which instilled in me a love for art. Art became my
career. I taught secondary art for thirty-nine years! I met my soul
mate in college, and we became inseparable. God gifted me with an
incredible man, and we have two beautiful children, inside and out.
I know His wish for me is to be blessed by Him, and I find such
comfort in his all-abiding love.

He has provided for me spiritually beyond measure, continually
sending me *Godwinks*.

He provides me with a sense of peace and strength through
my ever-growing body of friends. There is always a bird, a flower, a
rainbow to notice, and God provides me with joy!

Song: "My Wish" by Rascal Flatts

Action Step: Reread Numbers 6:24–26. Write down some ways God has been gracious to you.

_____

_____

_____

_____

_____

PRAYER

My wish for you is a prayer that You know Jesus, the Savior of your soul. May the grace of the Lord Jesus be with your spirit. In Jesus's Name.
Amen

GSUS CAN

Now when He got into a boat, His disciples followed Him. And suddenly a great tempest arose on the sea, so that the boat was covered with the waves. But He was asleep. Then His disciples came to Him and awoke Him, saying, "Lord, save us! We are perishing!" But He said to them, "Why are you fearful, O you of little faith?" Then He arose and rebuked the winds and the sea, and there was a great calm. So the men marveled, saying, "Who can this be, that even the winds and the sea obey Him?"

Matthew 8:23-27

*J*ESUS CAN HANDLE OUR STORMS. In this passage of Scripture, Jesus and His disciples are met with a great storm that rocked their boat. Just like the disciples, we face storms in our lives, but there is a sweet relief in knowing that Jesus can calm them.

In 2018, our five-year-old granddaughter contracted Kawasaki disease, an inflammatory illness that affects children under the age of five. She spent several days in the isolation wing of Columbus Children's Hospital. While driving home one day, I saw the license plate, GSUS CAN, which encouraged me. By seeing this message on the license plate, it reminded me that Jesus was with us and that he can help us through all of the seasons in our life. It was an awesome reminder to me that God is in control and that we need to have hope in all situations.

Our sweet Audrey made a full recovery and is a delight to our lives.

Song: "Jesus Can" by Mary Rice Hopkins

Action Step: Sometimes God answers our prayers in ways we never expected and we marvel at what He has done. What was a time in your life where you prayed for God to help and He did it in a way you never expected?

_____

_____

_____

_____

_____

PRAYER

*O Lord, I look to You when I see no way.
You make a way, and You can do anything but fail.
Help me trust You to do the impossible.
Amen*

BLSNG ME

You make known to me the path of life; you will fill
me with joy in your presence, with eternal pleasures
at your right hand.

Psalm 16:11

I WAS ON A BIKE RIDE and stopped for lunch along the path. BLSNG ME reminded me of all the simple enjoyment God gives us, like a bike ride through His creation.

This happened at just the right time to draw me back to God, while I was searching for peace during a difficult time. John 6:68 says, "Simon Peter answered him, 'Lord, to whom shall we go? You have the words of eternal life.'" I was seeking God in this season of my life, knowing He is the only one who could provide what I needed.

I thought of Philippians 4:8:

Finally, brothers and sisters, whatever is true, whatever is noble, whatever is right, whatever is pure, whatever is lovely, whatever is admirable—if anything is excellent or praiseworthy—think about such things.

God provides daily blessings that are pure, lovely, admirable. Many times, I am distracted and miss those daily blessings. Taking time and slowing down to look for God's blessings and think on them will remind us of His love for us.

Song: "The Lord Is Blessing Me" by Bishop Larry Trotter and Sweet Holy Spirit

Action Step: Take a break from your regular routine today to search for God's blessings. Maybe a quick walk outside or a peek out your window. Glance around and see what He provides in your daily surroundings.

_____

_____

_____

_____

_____

PRAYER

Thank You, Lord, for blessing me beyond what I deserve. You are able to bless me abundantly so that in all things, at all times, I have all I need to abound in every good work.
Amen

GD KNOWS

*Your servant Joab did this to change the present
situation. My lord has wisdom like that of an angel of
God—he knows everything that happens in the land.*

2 Samuel 14:20

WHEN I WAS KITTY'S BIBLE study leader, she told me how she would take notice of Christian license plates, so I started paying attention and found a number of them, just when I needed their messages myself.

When I was on the phone with my son one day, I saw the plate, GOD NOZ. Later, I saw Kitty in the parking lot at the grocery store. She called out to me and came over to my car. She was feeling down and dealing with anxiety. She wanted to talk about possibly leaving our Bible study group. When I told her about seeing that license plate, she said the name of one of her books was, *He Knows*.

A year later, Kitty was passing a church, and when she turned to look at the beautiful church building, two vehicles were there and she could see one of the plates: GOD NOZ. The same plate I had seen the year before. She stopped and took a picture. Wow, how God works to confirm His plans!

God knew how to encourage Kitty through that license plate, and she stayed with us in our Bible study. *GOD NOZ* how to encourage you too.

Song: "Does God Know All Things?" by Dana Dirksen

Action Step: Sometimes it can feel like God is too busy to know the details of our lives and the things that concern us. But He knows it all. And He knows us and what we need, even before we ask. Pay attention today to how God might be wanting to use you to encourage someone else with a kind word or action. Ask Him to show you His plan.

_____

_____

_____

_____

_____

PRAYER

Dear God, thank You, for we know You know us intimately. You love us with an everlasting love.
Amen

EMPOWRD

I can do all this [which He has called me to do]
through him who gives me strength.

Philippians 4:13

FOUR AND A HALF YEARS ago, my husband passed away. At that time, I believed I could not accomplish much of anything without him. I literally worshiped the ground he walked on! I had even told him, "I cannot do this life without you!"

But when he passed away, I turned to the Lord and prayed for His guidance and help to trust in Him. In the days, weeks, and now years since my husband passed, I have accomplished more than I ever thought possible. It is amazing to me how God has put things into place for me. I know He has a plan for my life or I would not still be here. In my weakness, God empowered me to serve Him in ways I could not do on my own. I now go forward with God's strength and empowerment.

Song: "Reborn Empowered" by Living Sacrifice

Action Step: Is there an area of your life that you feel weak in, unable to do what you need, what God has called you to do? Talk to God about it.

_____

_____

_____

_____

_____

PRAYER

Jesus, when I am weak, You are strong. When I say I can't, You always make a way. You tell us we are mountain movers, and I pray for Your mighty strength today.
Amen

AMZG GOD

And I am certain that God, who began the good work within you, will continue his work until it is finally finished on the day when Christ Jesus returns.

Philippians 1:6 NLT

JOHN AND I HAVE BEEN married forty-nine years, and I have just now come to the realization, "Only an amazing God!" Only an amazing God could take a know-it-all only child and a boss-of-the-mob firstborn of seven and keep them together. It is because He has made us His new creations (2 Corinthians 5:17), and He has never stopped working to conform us in our humanness into the image of His Son.

This year has been amazing in moving us toward more of what God has intended all along for our marriage. Because of the circumstances in our world, we have been relying more on each other and God. He has begun to heal us of our dysfunctional ways of relating to each other. But the holidays threw us into a tailspin. And the Enemy of our souls used it to cause conflict between us.

Because of our continual arguments about how to celebrate, darkness descended upon my soul. I couldn't hear God, and I couldn't think kindly of John and his motives. To my prayer chair I went to seek the Lord.

He revealed that the Enemy was at work. So I renounced the lies I was believing and affirmed God's truth about John and myself— we are beloved children of God, we are unconditionally loved and accepted by Him, we are called to Himself for a purpose, and we are secure in Him against all our enemies.

The darkness lifted. And I could again thank my amazing God for my husband who continued to love and care for me . . . only because of our AMAZING GOD!

Songs: "Amazing God" by William Murphy and "Amazing God" by Lincoln Brewster

Action Step: How has God used a conflict with another person to reveal His truth about them?

_____

_____

_____

_____

_____

PRAYER

You are an amazing God who shows us amazing grace.
We thank and praise You for Your grace, love, mercy,
and presence with us always.
Amen

GDZ GR8

Great is the Lord! He is most worthy of praise!
No one can measure his greatness.

Psalm 145:3 NLT

THESE LICENSE PLATES ARE REFRESHING to see. The more we emphasize how good or great God is, the less of a cynical or blaming attitude we will have toward Him.

In my six-year-plus cancer journey so far, I say, life is hard! Personal choices or mistakes make life happen to us. Get mad at life, but stay gracious and thankful toward God. Why? Because He ultimately created us, knows us, and loves us.

When I was diagnosed with cancer, I was mad at God, and it made my prayer time with Him awkward and not genuine. It is only human to question or get frustrated with God, yes! Talk with Him about your anger and your fears. He is big enough to handle it all. And in the process, He will teach you more about how much He loves you and will use hard things to bring you closer to Him.

Lean into your faith and love for God. Trust Him to walk with you through hard things. The psalmist David experienced hard things in his life. Some were consequences of his own bad choices; others were results of others' bad choices toward him. Each time, he cried out to God to ask for His help and also to praise God for what He already had done in his life.

When life gets hard and bad things happen, go to God and praise Him for what He has done in your life and tell him all about your current situation, knowing He will walk you through it, seeing you to the other side.

Song: "Very Great God" by Franklin Delano Williams

Action Step: Read through Psalm 145, and then pray it to God. Then write down some things God has done in your life that you can praise Him for.

_____

_____

_____

_____

_____

PRAYER

God, You are great and most worthy of our praise. We praise You for Your love, mercy, and grace, asking that You help us love others and show them mercy and grace as You do to us.
Amen

GODZWRK

Whatever you do, work heartily, as for the Lord
and not for men, knowing that from the Lord you
will receive the inheritance as your reward. You are
serving the Lord Christ.

Colossians 3:23-24 ESV

WHAT COMES TO MIND WHEN you hear or see the phrase, "God's work"? Possibly His mighty creations in nature, a beautiful babe in your arms, or a serving mission you are thinking of going on?

The Bible has much to say about God's work. We learn God has a say in what we work at, the resources for our work, our abilities and talents we need to do our work, and who we work for. He is the Creator of all of it, and we are His greatest work, His masterpiece (Ephesians 2:10). As His masterpiece, we were created to work like our God.

In Exodus 25–27, God has a careful plan for building the tabernacle and everything in it where He will reside with His people, the Israelites. On careful study, we can decipher God's attention to every detail. In Exodus 35–38, Moses led the people to build it exactly as God commanded.

On this side of the cross, we are God's tabernacle, and He dwells within us. And He certainly gave attention to every detail when He made us. As we go about our work, may we dwell on God's model for work and work with all our hearts for Him.

Song: "A Great Work" by Brian Courtney Wilson

Action Step: Read through Exodus 25–27 and notice the details of God's plans for the tabernacle, the place where He dwelt with His people before Christ came. Now read Psalm 139:1–18 and see the detail God put into creating each one of us, where He dwells now when we invite Him in. What amazes you the most about God's work?

_____

_____

_____

_____

_____

PRAYER

God, You are great and most worthy of our praise. We praise You for Your love, mercy, and grace, asking that You help us love others and show them mercy and grace as You do to us.
Amen

GOD B4 US

What, then, shall we say in response to these things?
If God is for us, who can be against us?

Romans 8:31

WE SOMETIMES FIND OURSELVES ALONE in the car or shower or on a day when all of our family is out of the house. Alone time can be good, but sometimes we can feel alone in a crowded room where we don't know anyone, or alone in our beliefs when they are different from those around us. And in those times, being alone can feel pretty bad. But God is always with us, always! He created us for community, and He promises to never leave us (Hebrews 13:5).

When the Israelites traveled through the wilderness, Exodus 13:21–22 tells us God went before them in a pillar of cloud by day and a pillar of fire at night to give them light. He never left them, and He will never leave us.

I can only imagine how afraid the Israelites must have been to leave their home and follow Moses into the wilderness, not knowing where they were going or how they would survive. Everything was new, and while they had each other, they often complained of feeling abandoned by God. Yet they had to trust God to lead them. And He did.

God went before them, and He goes before us. We can trust Him.

Song: "Everlasting God" by Lincoln Brewster

Action Step: Have you ever felt alone and afraid? Write about the experience. Read Romans 8:38–39. Is there anything that can separate us from God and His love? How does that encourage you?

_____

_____

_____

_____

_____

PRAYER

God, if You are for us, who can be against us? We thank You that nothing can separate us from Your love and that there is no condemnation for those in Christ Jesus.
Amen

ACTS 18

But you will receive power when the Holy Spirit
comes on you; and you will be my witnesses in
Jerusalem, and in all Judea and Samaria, and to the
ends of the earth.

Acts 1:8

*W*HEN WE RECEIVE CHRIST AS our Savior and we believe our Father in heaven is three in one—Father, Son and Holy Spirit—we receive a free gift with which no other could compare. With the Holy Spirit in you, if you ever feel lonely, remember you are never alone. Weakness is overcome by the power of the Holy Spirit. Wisdom is discerning by the call of the Holy Spirit.

The Holy Spirit is our helper, our sanctifier, our leader to Christ, and our giver of gifts. If we remember to call upon God, the Holy Spirit activates in our soul and fills us with all the inheritance we received as children of God.

Try an experiment and spend one day calling upon the Holy Spirit in all you do, in every hour of the day. Share your feelings and ask for help. Activate His power within you.

Song: "Ye Shall Be Witnesses" by Ruthie Atlanta

Action Step: As you spend a day calling on the Holy Spirit in all you do, record your experiences here.

_____

_____

_____

_____

_____

PRAYER

Holy Spirit, oh how I love You. Thank You for living with me and never leaving me alone. Thank You for guiding me and helping me. Let my words be pleasing to You, always.
Amen

2 DREAM

In the last days, God says, I will pour out my Spirit on all people. Your sons and daughters will prophesy, your young men will see visions, your old men will dream dreams.

Acts 2:17

*I*N BIBLICAL TIMES, GOD GAVE dreams to many people in both the Old and New Testaments. Some dreams/visions are for us and God alone. Others are messages God gives us to share with others to encourage them.

I have memories of being at an elementary school friend's home, and her record player was playing over and over, "The Impossible Dream."

These words remind me of Jesus and what He did for us. He beat death. And because of His victory over death, His disciples went on to give up their lives for the gospel, the good news of eternal life in Christ. Paul the apostle was a martyr for Jesus as well, obedient to His cause until death. And in Acts 1:8 in the final days, for those of us who have received the Holy Spirit, God will give us dreams and visions to speak to us, encourage us, and lead us to carry out the mission was have been called to partner with Him in, to tell others about the love of God and eternal life through Christ His Son.

Some days this may feel like an impossible dream, but with God, all things are possible (Matthew 19:26).

Song: "The Impossible Dream" by Jackie Evancho

Action Step: Have you ever had a dream or a vision that you were certain was from God? How did you respond? Write about it here.

_____

_____

_____

_____

_____

PRAYER

Dearest God, thank You for all the dreams You have given us. Dreams of the past, present, and future. You gave so many dreams to those in the Old and New Testaments. We praise You, God.

Amen

GODS WRD

So is my word that goes out from my mouth: It will not return to me empty, but will accomplish what I desire and achieve the purpose for which I sent it.

Isaiah 55:11

*I*SEE THIS LICENSE PLATE AROUND town a lot. I used to be in God's Word all the time, almost daily, and the plate would remind me to get into His Word. When we learn and keep God's Word in our hearts and minds, things change in our lives and the lives of others, our prayer life improves, and so does life itself. There is power in God's Word, power in speaking it out loud and sharing it with others. It will never return void.

For a season, I was not in God's Word faithfully, and I noticed a difference. When I rejoined BSF and got in the Word again, my anxiety eased. God's Word is our daily bread, feeding us the nutrients our bodies and souls need to thrive.

Psalm 119 reminds us how God's Word brings wisdom and understanding, helping us better know the heart of our Father.

Song: "God's Word" by Bryann Trejo

Action Step: Take time to read Psalm 119, even just a portion of it. What do you notice about God's Word?

_____

_____

_____

_____

_____

PRAYER

God, Your Word is all God-breathed and endures forever. Help us not just listen to Your Word but do what it says. Amen

SECTION 5

FORGIVENESS

FORGIVEN

*Then Peter came to Jesus and asked, "Lord, how
many times shall I forgive my brother or sister who
sins against me? Up to seven times?"
Jesus answered, "I tell you, not seven times, but
seventy-seven times.*

Matthew 18:21–22

WHEN PETER ASKS JESUS HOW many times must he forgive his brother, Peter thinks he is giving Jesus a high number when he asks, "Up to seven times?" In Rabbinic teaching, an offended person only needed to forgive someone three times.

When Jesus tells Peter, "seventy times seven," He really means infinitely. There are no limits on forgiveness. Forgiveness keeps our hearts soft toward others and frees us from the burden of the offense.

Forgiving does not mean forgetting. Some of us have experienced grievous sins against us, our loved ones, and friends. God and Jesus help us to forgive when we ask, but our minds cannot always forget. The Holy Spirit will help us to pray for those who have hurt us and our loved ones, and to also pray a blessing over them as Jesus commands us to do in Matthew 5:44. This is not always immediate. Sometimes forgiveness takes time. In doing so, we begin to heal from the pain and hurt, even though scars remain.

Song: "Forgiven" by David Crowder

Action Step: Forgiveness is not easy, but oh how wonderful to be forgiven! Have you ever received forgiveness from someone? How did you feel? Carry that feeling with you the next time you need to forgive someone.

_____

_____

_____

_____

_____

PRAYER

Jesus, bless You for forgiving our sins—past, present, and future—when we come to You and accept You as our Lord and Savior. We can never thank You enough for what You did for us all. Leaving heaven and dying on the cross for us. We are forever blessed.
Amen

4GIVNES

Therefore, my friends, I want you to know that
through Jesus the forgiveness of sins is
proclaimed to you.

Acts 13:38

WHEN I WAS YOUNG, I would go to confession because that is what I was taught, and I would confess my sins to a priest. But when I got older, I wanted to confess directly to God and Jesus.

When I became a born-again Christian, I learned that Jesus is our high priest (Hebrews 4:14), and because He gave His life to forgive our sins, we can go directly and confidently to God the Father to receive forgiveness.

One day in church, many sins I had not confessed came to my mind; tears were flowing, and I could not stop crying. I was overwhelmed with gratitude that I had been forgiven for all my sins.

We can ask people to forgive us, too, when we hurt them so the relationship can be restored. But it is God who purifies us from all our sin; regardless of whether the other person forgives us, we are forgiven. Thankfully, my heavenly Father gives forgiveness to all who believe Jesus is their Savior and confess, pray, ask, even cry to Him to forgive them.

Song: "Forgiveness" by Matthew West

Action Step: Ask the Holy Spirit to search your heart to see if there is anything you need to confess to God. As you confess and seek forgiveness, also praise and thank God for His generous gift of forgiveness through His Son Jesus.

_____

_____

_____

_____

_____

<u>PRAYER</u>

Dearest God and Jesus, we thank You that we can go directly to You and ask for forgiveness for our sins.
Amen

2IRELND

*In the same way, I tell you, there is rejoicing
in the presence of the angels of God over
one sinner who repents.*

Luke 15:10

I HAD LUNCH ONE DAY WITH my brother Mike. His family had just taken a trip to Ireland, and he wanted to tell me about it.

He and our brother Jerry used to go almost yearly and stay at our relatives' farm. I once asked Mike if there was a favorite town in Ireland that he loved. Donegal was his favorite, and I told him Kerry and Dingle were mine.

As I was leaving the restaurant, I saw four license plates, one right after the other: DONEGAL, JC SINGS (Jesus sings), BLESSD, and 2IRELND.

All four license plates reminded me of one of my favorite places, Ireland. I am blessed to have been there three times in my life. I long to own my own home there someday in the breathtaking patchwork-quilt countryside. Oh, how it reminds me of what I hope heaven will be like!

I love the imagery of Jesus singing and the connection with the beautiful country of Ireland. It reminds me how when His sheep find Him, when wandering sheep return to Him, He will sing over them.

Song: "Home to Donegal" by Nathan Carter

Action Step: Is there a place you've visited or lived that you hope heaven will be like? In what ways?

_____

_____

_____

_____

_____

PRAYER

We all have countries where we and our ancestors were born. This means a lot of us, and I am grateful that Ireland was the place of my great grandparents and grandparents. Everything about us is important to God.
Amen

2ND CHNC

But while he was still a long way off, his father saw
him and was filled with compassion for him;
he ran to his son, threw his arms around him
and kissed him.

Luke 15:20

*O*H, HOW MANY CHANCES GOD and Jesus have given me! So much like the prodigal son, I have needed many second chances, and I will be forever grateful for getting them.

I think of the father of the prodigal son, looking and waiting, hoping for his son's return. As a parent, I can imagine the pain of wondering if my child will ever come home. As the child, I am ever too familiar with the fear of wondering, "Will my parent forgive me? Will I be accepted back and forgiven?"

In that culture, it was not the custom for the father to run to the rebellious child, but in this parable, Jesus paints a beautiful picture of our heavenly Father who loves us so much that He will do anything to have us back home with Him. When we sin, we never have to wonder or worry if we are loved and accepted by God.

He is waiting with open arms, and when we turn back to Him, He is quick to run to us, throw His arms around us, and kiss us.

Song: "Second Chance" by Hezekiah Walker

Action Step: Have you ever been afraid that God will reject you or stay angry with you when you sin against Him? Picture God as the father of the prodigal son, waiting and watching for you to return so He can run after you, embrace you, and welcome you home.

<u>PRAYER</u>

Dear Lord, thank You for giving us so many chances—
You give us more than we deserve, and we are indebted to
You for Your never-ending forgiveness.
Amen

SECTION 6

FAITH

B LYK HIM

See what great love the Father has lavished on us,
that we should be called children of God! . . .
Dear friends, now we are children of God, and what
we will be has not yet been made known. But we
know that when Christ appears, we shall be like him,
for we shall see him as he is.

1 John 3:1-2

WE ALL NEED TO MAKE a concentrated effort in our lives to be imitators of Jesus. His desire is for no one to perish but for each of us to come to salvation through faith in Him. Life is not easy, and trying to love like Him can prove very difficult. It helps our minds to focus by getting alone to talk and pray to our heavenly Father like Jesus did. We also need to be still and listen.

Our lives are so cluttered with noise and distractions. Isn't it strange how we can spend hours watching television and then feel there is only a ten-minute slot in our daily routine for the Lord?

Blessings will always follow obedience. It is definitely worth our time as the reward is great and covered with joy and contentment.

Song: "It Won't Be Long" by Andrae Crouch & The Disciples

Action Step: For the next twenty-four hours, write down everything you do throughout the day and how much time it takes. Where might you find some time to devote to God instead?

_____

_____

_____

_____

_____

PRAYER

God, let me be free of judgment toward others, and do not allow me to put myself higher than another. Open my heart to see a need instead of turning a blind eye.

Amen

CRST 1ST

Jesus replied, "Love the Lord your God with all your heart and with all your soul and with all your mind."

Matthew 22:37

HE FIRST AND GREATEST COMMANDMENT is to love God. We need to remember to put God first in all we do. It is difficult at times, especially when we feel like God is not giving us an answer, but if we wait on God, God is there for us. Our heavenly Father never gives up on us. Always be ready and willing to pray at the moment, anything that pertains to Christ and to others.

A few of us went out to dinner after Bible study one night, and we saw this plate. Kitty always puts Christ first in her life, no matter the situation. Kitty and I have been there for each other through praying prayers of comfort, mailing cards, letters, and more. We both lost brothers in 2010. Putting Christ first is being in His Word, taking Bible studies, and living it out by showing Christ to others and not just talking about Him. It is sharing all that Jesus has done for us.

Song: "First" by Lauren Daigle

Action Step: Think of someone you know that puts Christ first in their life. What specific actions does this person do that shows you Christ is first?

_____

_____

_____

_____

_____

PRAYER

God, we need to put You first. Help me to continue to put You first in my life.
Amen

HEISLRD

If you declare with your mouth "Jesus is Lord," and believe in your heart that God raised him from the dead, you will be saved.

Romans 10:9

*H*E IS LORD. SO SIMPLE a phrase with so mighty a power may have never been!

Some people can go to church for years without knowing in their hearts if they will go to heaven when they die. But the Bible promises that we will indeed, by faith and by God's grace if we simply believe in the Lord. Simply beautiful.

Jesus Christ is my Lord and Savior, and I am forever grateful and indebted to Him for turning this wandering sheep back in to His fold and loving arms. He drew me to Himself like He drew my brother Jerry into His loving embrace. I look forward to that day I see Jesus face-to-face and finally see our heavenly Father.

When I have felt alone and in the depths of despair, Jesus came along and pulled me out of the pit, and He wants to do the same for you. He is the source of joy and contentment. Is Jesus Lord over your life?

Song: "He Is Lord" by Elevation Worship

Action Step: Is Jesus Lord over your life? Why or why not?

_____

_____

_____

_____

_____

PRAYER

"He is Lord; He is Lord," sings my soul. You have risen from the dead, my Lord and Savior—Lord of my life.
Amen

ARMOR GD

Take the helmet of salvation and the sword of the
Spirit, which is the word of God.

Ephesians 6:17

WE WOULD NEVER THINK OF leaving our home half-dressed, but often we neglect to put on our spiritual clothing. Paul tells us in Ephesians that we have a responsibility to stand against spiritual wickedness and to meet our adversaries head on. When we submit our will to God's, He fills us with faith and the power to pull down the Enemy's strongholds. God supplies all the armor needed to fight the Enemy, but we have to put it on!

Many times, we fight battles with our emotions, but Ephesians teaches us we need to battle the spiritual forces that attack our emotions. Before venting our feelings in the flesh, we must be willing to surrender to the power of the Holy Spirit.

In order to be effective, we must always be ready to share why we believe in Jesus Christ while living a life of integrity.

My favorite "piece" of armor is the sword of the Spirit because it shares the message of salvation that Jesus Christ came to save us and give us abundant life.

Song: "Onward, Christian Soldiers" by Sabine Baring-Gould

Action Step: Read Ephesians 6:10–18, the armor of God. What is your favorite piece of armor? Why?

_____

_____

_____

_____

_____

PRAYER

Lord, You tell us in Your Word to put on the armor of God. When we do, we can tell the evil one to leave. Praise You, Lord, for Your Word.
Amen

JC IS KNG

"You are a king, then!" said Pilate.
Jesus answered, "You say that I am a king. In fact,
the reason I was born and came into the world is
to testify to the truth. Everyone on the side of truth
listens to me."

John 18:37

As I was driving a friend to my house, I prayed to let us see a Jesus/Christian license plate. The Lord let us see the perfect plate, JC IS KNG—Jesus Christ is King. We have known each other for over twenty years and lean on each other for strength.

She has an autistic son whose life has led her to spend many hours in prayer and make some difficult decisions as his advocate. We have prayed for each other's families, which has truly sealed our friendship. We have come to lean on each other as prayer partners as well. Our friendship reminds me of the song "Lean On Me" by Bill Withers. That is what we do!

Yes, our Lord is the King. My friend and I are proof of this. My friend and I are proof of His goodness and mercy.

Song: "What A Beautiful Name" by Hillsong Worship

Action Step: Who in your life do you lean on? How do you and your friend encourage each other to keep Jesus Christ as your King?

_____

_____

_____

_____

_____

PRAYER

*Jesus, You are King of Kings, Lord of Lords.
May we live our lives submitted to Your authority
as Your faithful children.
Amen*

JMJ WWJD

"What do you want me to do for you?" Jesus asked him. The blind man said, "Rabbi, I want to see."

Mark 10:51

A COUPLE OF WEEKS AGO, I met the owners of the "Jesus, Mary, and Joseph . . . What Would Jesus Do" license plate. They are in my prayer group, and they have both prayed for me and over me. I am blessed to have heard their stories and thankful to God for placing them in my life.

When I saw this plate, my first thought was, *I know exactly what that means.* It brought back the memory of my Irish Catholic grandmother O'Sullivan. She would always say, "Jesus, Mary, and Joseph," and then pray the rosary throughout the entire day and evening. It was such a wonderful memory of her.

When thinking about the years I wore the WWJD bracelets, I admit I didn't always think about what Jesus would do. I might be thinking instead, *What would Kitty do?* Later I found it best to look to Jesus as my source. What Would Jesus Do? Throughout Scripture, we see Him leading with love, always doing the will of His Father. By spending daily time in prayer with God, Jesus received strength and wisdom to always walk in love. And we are called to do the same.

Song: "What Would Jesus Do" by Adam Gregory

Action Step: Think about a current struggle in your life. If someone asked you, "What would Jesus do?" what might you say?

_____

_____

_____

_____

_____

PRAYER

Dearest Jesus, we need to live to be more like You. We need people to see us as Jesus—loving, truthful, gracious, merciful, and more.

Amen

11 MRCLS

Jesus said to the servants, "Fill the jars with water";
so they filled them to the brim. Then he told them,
"Now draw some out and take it to the master of the
banquet." They did so, and the master of the banquet
tasted the water that had been turned into wine.
He did not realize where it had come from, though
the servants who had drawn the water knew. Then
he called the bridegroom aside and said, "Everyone
brings out the choice wine first and then the cheaper
wine after the guests have had too much to drink;
but you have saved the best till now."

John 2:7-10

*S*HORTLY BEFORE MY DAUGHTER'S WEDDING, we had news that my father had been admitted to the ICU, and we didn't know whether he would ever come home again. In the next two months, I had a daughter graduating from high school and the other from college, with her wedding the following week.

During the second week of my father's illness, my mother was told she needed open-heart surgery immediately. Emotionally, my mother was a wreck and begged the doctor to wait until the situation with Dad was over. Money was tight as neither I nor my mother were working during this time. I was not sure how to handle all this, and then God moved in.

My father passed away. Mom was rechecked, and it was decided she no longer needed surgery. The doctor said he could not understand it because the testing showed only 10 percent blockage where it had previously shown 90 percent.

We belonged to a Bible study and one night someone said, "Prayer is wonderful, but God calls us to do things that are practical also."

They had a dinner for everyone and presented us with a check within pennies of my six weeks' wages. The next few weeks melted together, and I felt like I floated through them.

I will always be grateful for the friends He put in our life. God really does care about every detail, and He still works miracles.

Song: "He Still Does (Miracles)" by Hawk Nelson

Action Step: Have you ever experienced an unexplainable moment? Journal about it. How might God have been revealing Himself to you?

_____

_____

_____

_____

_____

PRAYER

Jesus, Lord of miracles, we thank You that as You walked on earth and did wondrous deeds, that you are still a God of miracles today.
Amen

24 JESUS

*You will keep in perfect peace those whose minds are
steadfast, because they trust in you.
Trust in the L*ORD *forever, for the L*ORD,
*the L*ORD *himself, is the Rock eternal.*

Isaiah 26:3-4

*I*WAS LEAVING A LOCAL GROCERY store when I ran into a woman I recognized. We locked eyes, so I knew she was thinking the same thing. All of sudden it clicked. We knew each other from a small boutique that sold hand-painted furniture and home decor. We didn't know each other well, but we knew enough to keep the conversation going. She said she no longer worked there but added that she needed to find a job that paid more. I could tell she was struggling without her giving me a lot of details, and before we departed, I asked her if I could pray over her. She said yes.

I drove home with a heavy heart thinking about her and wondering, *Did I give her enough time? Was I good listener? Did she need more from me?*

I turned left at the light, and as I was making the turn, I saw a license plate that read, 24 JESUS. It reminded me of today's Scripture: "You will keep in perfect peace those whose minds are steadfast, because they trust in you. Trust in the LORD forever, for the LORD, the LORD himself, is the Rock eternal" (Isaiah 26:3–4).

This license plate, along with running into this woman I knew, reminded me to keep my heart, mind, and soul focused on Jesus.

Song: "Stand in Faith" by Danny Gokey

Action Step: What are some things that distract you from keeping your mind on Christ? Write them down and ask God to help you shift your focus to Him and His peace.

_____

_____

_____

_____

_____

PRAYER

Jesus, we all need You twenty-four hours a day every day. Help us to be closer to You, to love and need You more. Help us to act more like You.
Amen

BI F8TH

By faith we understand that the universe was
formed at God's command, so that what is seen was
not made out of what was visible.

Hebrews 11:3

*H*EBREWS 11 IS FULL OF inspiring "by faith" stories. Past, present, and future, we walk by faith with our heavenly Father and our Lord Jesus Christ. The Holy Spirit lives inside us to enable us to fully walk by faith. At times, as humans, we stumble in our faith walk, and the Trinity is there to help us keep going.

Hebrews 11 tells of faithful followers who obeyed God even when they could not see His plan or why He was asking them to do what He did. His instructions might have seemed crazy to them, completely unreasonable.

Noah, out of obedience to God and by faith, built an ark even thought he had never seen rain, much less a flood. By faith, the Israelites marched around Jericho and blew trumpets because God told them He would help them take the city this way. By faith, Abraham went to another land without knowing where he was going.

By faith, Rahab the prostitute believed God would protect her because she helped His men.

Our faith pleases God, and He promises to reward us as we put our hope in a better life after resurrection when we are with Him for eternity.

Song: "By Faith (Live)" by Keith & Kristyn Getty

Action Step: Have you ever experienced a time when God asked you to do something that didn't make sense, may have even seemed crazy? How did you respond? Read through Hebrews 11. How does this chapter inspire you?

_____

_____

_____

_____

_____

PRAYER

*Abba Father, You draw so many people to yourself
and to Jesus, and by faith we accept Your invitation
to be Jesus followers.
Amen*

HIMB4ME

Seek his will in all you do,
and he will show you which path to take.

Proverbs 3:6 NLT

E MUST PUT GOD FIRST above everything else. Put Jesus first before anything else. When I saw this license plate, HIMB4ME, it brought to mind to stick with God.

In Denzel Washington's commencement speech at Dillard University, "Put God First," he encouraged his audience, "Put God first in everything you do. Everything I have is by the grace of God."

How can we put God first?

- Talk to Him.
- Pray for others, our world, and all future generations.
- Read and memorize His Word.
- Do a Bible study with others or by yourself. There are many great resources available today.
- Go to a church; listen to a sermon online or on the radio.

- Help others in need; give of your time for Him. Give food and clothing to those who need it.

Below is the link to listen.
https://www.youtube.com/watch?v=BxY_eJLBflk&feature=youtu.be

Song: "A Man You Would Write About" by 4HIM

Action Step: How can you put God first today? Write it down.

_____

_____

_____

_____

_____

PRAYER

Lord, help me with every task I have in front of me this day, to do it all to Your glory. Let me serve others with a cheerful heart and remember You first in all the day brings.
Amen

HIS BOOK

In the beginning was the Word, and the Word was with God, and the Word was God.

John 1:1

*L*ET'S SPEND MORE TIME IN *His* book than on Facebook. Instead of posting, let's pray. Instead of scrolling, let's read Scripture. For many years, I owned a Bible but I only opened it when it was time for Bible study or there was a need.

This license plate, HIS BOOK, reminds me of the Apostle John's message that Jesus is the Word, and He was with God from the very beginning of time, and He is with us too. Jesus is the living book who came to earth to show us how to live and love others, and by reading His words in Scripture and spending time meditating on those words, we can learn to follow in His steps.

Song: "Books of the Bible" by North Point Kids and "Speak the Word" by Tina Campbell with Teddy Campbell

Action Step: Read through Psalm 1. What does this Scripture say about the word of the Lord? How does this encourage you?

_____

_____

_____

_____

_____

PRAYER

*O Lord, Your book is Your love story to us and a lamp
unto our feet. Help us to taste and see how good Your Word
is and live our lives as You have taught us to do.
Amen*

BLD 4 HM

Therefore, since we have such a hope,
we are very bold.

2 Corinthians 3:12

ONE DAY WHILE I WAS driving around town, a car in front of me had a license plate that read BLD 4 HM (Bold For Him). They also had a bumper sticker, "2 Corinthians 3:12."

It said to me, do not be afraid to show your faith in God, and in fact, be bold in your faith. We were created for God's glory and to spend time with Him just as we desire our children to spend time with us. As He infuses us with love and boldness, we find ourselves doing things that bring Him pleasure and joy.

For me, being bold for Him looks like helping with catechism classes at church so the younger generation knows about the Bible and the Trinity (God, Jesus, and the Holy Spirit). In my home, I boldly display my beliefs through sayings and objects of my faith, like the crucifix, and I give donations to different groups.

Song: "Bold" by Grace and Corey Scarlett

Action Step: Because of your hope in Christ and what He has done for you, in what ways can you be bold in your faith?

_____

_____

_____

_____

_____

<u>PRAYER</u>

Dearest Jesus, because You were bold for us,
we will be bold for You.
Amen

BLESS ME

But blessed is the one who trusts in the Lᴏʀᴅ,
whose confidence is in Him.

Jeremiah 17:7

*M*Y HUSBAND AND I WERE pulling in to the cancer center on the morning of my breast cancer surgery when I spotted a license plate that said, BLESS ME. I not only noticed because my friend had me on the lookout, but because it spoke to me that morning. It blessed me as I remembered the Lord telling me He was protecting me before I found out I even had breast cancer.

I was sitting in the cancer center for a repeat mammogram imaging when I clearly heard through the Spirit, *I am protecting you, Christine.* I very seldom hear "Christine" unless it is from my Lord. It so happened that they found another area of suspicion in addition to the original area of concern, and I had an ultrasound on both sites. It was determined I needed a biopsy or maybe two. The morning of the biopsy there was a debate if one area needed biopsied or not. It was decided to do both and thanks be to God! He did protect and BLESS ME, because the site they almost did *not* biopsy was the one that was malignant; the other was not!

I also have been truly blessed through this cancer journey by so many friends who have prayed for me, encouraged me, sent cards, and called me. May you, dear reader, be blessed as I have been, even with cancer!

> The Lord bless you and keep you; the LORD make his face shine on you and be gracious to you; the LORD turn his face toward you and give you peace. (Numbers 6:24–26)

Songs: "Blessings" by Laura Story and "The Blessing" by Kari Jobe and Cody Carnes

Action Step: List some ways God has blessed you.

_____

_____

_____

_____

_____

PRAYER

Sovereign Lord, You bless us in so many ways. May You give us the eyes to see those blessings and give You thanks and praise.

Amen

CALLED

*To this he called you through our gospel, so that you
may obtain the glory of our Lord Jesus Christ.*

2 Thessalonians 2:14 ESV

WE ARE ALL CALLED. CALLED to give to others the hope we have in Jesus Christ our Lord. Do you ever feel like only pastors and priests are called to serve God? I did. Yet Scripture tells us over and over we are *all* called. But to what are we called?

To a holy life:

He has saved us and called us to a holy life—not because of anything we have done but because of his own purpose and grace. This grace was given us in Christ Jesus before the beginning of time. (2 Timothy 1:9)

To fellowship with Jesus:

God is faithful, who has called you into fellowship with his Son, Jesus Christ our Lord. (1 Corinthians 1:9)

Out of darkness:

But you are a chosen people, a royal priesthood, a holy nation, God's special possession, that you may declare the praises of him who called you out of darkness into his wonderful light. (1 Peter 2:9)

I realize now that to be called by God is the process by which God draws a person to Himself to have a relationship with Him. It's an invitation for God to open our minds to spiritual truth and salvation. An invitation to be called into His family as a Christian and into the book of life.

Song: "Called" by Avalon

Action Step: Read Ephesians 4. Describe what the apostle Paul means when he says, "I urge you to live a life worthy of the calling you have received" in verse 1.

_____

_____

_____

_____

_____

PRAYER

Sovereign Lord, You bless us in so many ways. May You give us the eyes to see those blessings and give You thanks and praise.

Amen

MAN 4 GOD

But you, man of God, flee from all this, and pursue righteousness, godliness, faith, love, endurance and gentleness.

1 Timothy 6:11

S A MAN WHO IS constantly looking to God for guidance and direction, I have been led to the reality that my faith in God is well placed. Being a man of God isn't believing that one is perfect and without sin. To the contrary, being a man of God is accepting my imperfections and sinfulness like God does. God knows of our human failings and accepts them. God, while knowing of our weakness and sin, gives us the knowledge and information on how to lead man away from sin. Heaven isn't full of perfect people; it's full of people who by God's grace, have accepted Jesus as their Lord and Savior. A man of God believes that it is the goal to glorify God through his actions. That through his actions, without wearing his faith in God on his sleeve, people will see that he is a man of God, and will themselves be moved to become people of God.

Song: "Man of God" by Neil Diamond

Action Step: Reread 1 Timothy 6:11. Which of those characteristics can you pursue today? How?

_____

_____

_____

_____

_____

PRAYER

Oh Jesus, I am a man for God. I pray that I may live my life honoring You, oh Lord. Amen

ELOHIM

In the beginning God [Elohim] created
the heavens and the earth.

Genesis 1:1

*A*LOCAL RADIO STATION HAD A story from a male caller who stated that he would travel the wide road, not the narrow way to heaven. The very next day, miracles happened. He turned his life over to Jesus.

Elohim is one of the many names for God. It is found only in the Hebrew language, meaning Mighty Creator. It is the first name God calls Himself and occurs thirty-two times in the first chapter of Genesis. It is a plural form, recognizing the Trinity—Father, Son, and the Holy Spirit. (*The Names of God* by Ann Spangler, 2009.)

The owner of this plate is a local pastor, whom I've met many times, and whenever his car is near mine, it is often directly in front of my vehicle. This plate reminds me that I am made in the image of my Creator, and we are His masterpiece, created to do good works for Him to reflect His glory to the world.

Song: "Elohim" by Nathaniel Bassey

Action Step: Read Ephesians 2:10. What are some ways you reflect Creator God to the world around you?

_____

_____

_____

_____

_____

<u>PRAYER</u>

You are the one true living God who began all things
and has all authority and sovereignty.
We praise You for who You are!
Amen

DEUT111

Love the LORD your God and keep his requirements,
his decrees, his laws and his commands always.

Deuteronomy 11:1

WHILE ATTENDING AN ANNUAL CHRISTIAN concert with friends, I saw this license plate, which could be read as Deuteronomy 11:1 or Deuteronomy 1:11. Both verses encourage me. If we love the Lord our God and keep His requirements, then may the Lord, the God of our ancestors, increase us a thousand times and bless us as He has promised!

In Deuteronomy 11, God is reminding His people that it is because they were witnesses to His great miracles in the wilderness as they were freed from slavery in Egypt, and they must remember what they experienced and saw God do, obeying His laws so they will have the strength to take over the land God is giving them that they are crossing the Jordan River to possess (Deuteronomy 11:8). Oh, how many times I have witnessed God do miracles in my own life, and it is those miracles that give me the strength to obey His commands and keep going toward heaven, the land He is giving us to possess. Because *His* laws bring life. Oh, how God wants to bless us!

Song: "The Song of Moses" performed by Patricia A. Tyler

Action Step: Are there commands God has given that are harder for you to follow? Which one(s)? Why do you suppose these are hard to follow? Write down a miracle or two (an answered prayer) you have experienced God do in your life or one that a friend has told you about. How can that encourage you to follow God more closely?

_____

_____

_____

_____

_____

PRAYER

May the Lord save my loved ones
and bring the world to salvation in Jesus Christ.
Amen

FAITH

*Now faith is confidence in what we hope for and
assurance about what we do not see.*

Hebrews 11:1

AITH CAN MEAN DIFFERENT THINGS to all who see it: a girl's first name, faith that we get that much-needed job, faith in what we cannot see, touch, or hear. Also, faith can be related to a church sermon or some use of the term "spiritual thinking." It can even cause conflict for some who may see this plate.

Maybe they have been wanting to get "back" to their faith. They have been living life on their own and have been self-sufficient. They realize they need the true faith in our biblical God. It can also make an unbeliever think twice or even trigger a deep desire to have a faith or believe now in a higher power.

That's why it can be vital to share your faith graciously, because you never know when someone is seeking. Give them the opportunity to hear and choose.

Song: "Keep the Faith" by Bon Jovi

Action Step: What does faith mean to you?

_____

_____

_____

_____

_____

PRAYER

May my faith in You, O God, be hope to those around me, for without faith it is impossible to please You. In faith I believe You exist and reward those who earnestly seek You.

Amen

FLW TH SN

Then Jesus said to his disciples, "Whoever wants to be my disciple must deny themselves and take up their cross and follow me."

Matthew 16:24

JUST WHEN I WAS READY to cry about losing my brother, there would be FLW TH SN. I would be questioning God and Jesus about how and why my brother passed away. I knew a lot of why, but I did not understand why they did not save my brother. I knew he was finally at peace, but he left us all behind. Following Jesus was the only thing that I could do to survive. I would see it hundreds of times and just knew Jesus was speaking to me, telling me not to give up, to go on. My family and loved ones needed me.

It is because God is with me, carrying me at times and walking with me at times, that I am able to follow Him and go where He goes. He is the one who gives me the strength I need to keep going.

Song: "Follow The Son" by Hillsong Worship

Action Step: Has there been an experience in your life when you felt like you could not go on? What was it that nudged you to take that next small step to keep going? A loved one's kind words? A verse from Scripture? A song? Write about it.

_____

_____

_____

_____

_____

PRAYER

Lord, help us to follow Your Son, Jesus. Jesus, we trust in You. Help us to always come to You even if we stumble and stray. Bring us back to you.

Amen

FROG4ME

But now, O Lord, upon what am I relying?
You are my only hope!

Psalm 39:7 NET

FULLY RELY ON GOD. LORD, You tell us to rely, believe, and trust more in You. At times it is hard to do when circumstances are beyond our control, when we feel so overwhelmed by life.

If we pray to God to help us to fully rely on Him, He can help us in His time.

I was at BSF, and a woman parked next to me and asked, "Where did you find your stuffed frog on your car dashboard?" She explained she had a friend who was looking for a stuffed frog for her child.

I told the woman she could have mine; it was from a pet store. She was so surprised that I gave it to her. I also told her what F.R.O.G. meant and to share with her friend.

Song: "F.R.O.G (Fully Rely On God)" by BIG Ministries

Action Step: What is one area in your life where you need to fully rely on God? What might that look like?

_____

_____

_____

_____

_____

PRAYER

*Whatever I do, whether in word or in deed, may
I fully rely on You, my God, to direct my path and
trust You in hard times.*
Amen

FTH LV HP

And now these three remain: faith, hope and love.
But the greatest of these is love.

1 Corinthians 13:13

KITTY AND I OFTEN LAUGH at the license plates I see, versus the ones that she sees. I am grateful for the ones that we see together, like FTH LV HP (Faith, Love, Hope).

We were out shopping together and met the owner of this license plate. These three simple words stirred up emotions for me. Faith—Jesus is always with me. Love—I'm with people I care about who care about me. Hope—everything is going to be okay because I'm not in control.

First Corinthians 13 is often referred to as the Love Chapter in the Bible. Is describes love and how without it, our faith means nothing. Our hope means nothing.

Love is patient, love is kind. It does not envy, it does not boast,
it is not proud. It does not dishonor others, it is not self-seeking,
it is not easily angered, it keeps no record of wrongs. Love does

not delight in evil but rejoices with the truth. It always protects, always trusts, always hopes, always perseveres. Love never fails. (1 Corinthians 13:4–8)

God is love (1 John 4:16). It is because of His love for us and His great name that we worship Him.

Song: "What A Beautiful Name" by Hillsong Worship

Action Step: Look over the list of descriptions for love in 1 Corinthians 13:4–8. Which one do you want more of? And which one are you grateful for?

_____

_____

_____

_____

_____

PRAYER

Jesus, my faith in You carries me, my hope for You leads me, my love from You covers me completely. Thank You for Your unending love.
Amen

FOREVER

*For the Lord himself will come down from heaven,
with a loud command, with the voice of the
archangel and with the trumpet call of God, and the
dead in Christ will rise first. After that, we who are
still alive and are left will be caught up together with
them in the clouds to meet the Lord in the air. And so
we will be with the Lord forever.*

1 Thessalonians 4:16-17

SEEING THIS LICENSE PLATE REMINDED me I will be in heaven forever. As a child, when I would talk to my mom about heaven and being there forever, I got scared, and I remember asking, "What if I don't like heaven?" Forever is a long time to be somewhere you don't like!

My mom was reassuring that heaven would be a beautiful place. She would get on her knees with me, and we would pray together. From then on, heaven has been a place where I've looked forward to spending eternity.

I can't wait to go to heaven. I will see my loved ones there. Jesus promised me that He would save my family when my younger brother, Jerry, died.

Song: "Praise You Forever" by Marvin Sapp

Action Step: What do you think of when you think of heaven?

_____

_____

_____

_____

_____

PRAYER

Jesus, I will forever follow and trust in You.
Amen

GLORIFY

*You are the light of the world. A city set on a hill
cannot be hidden. Nor do people light a lamp and put
it under a basket, but on a stand, and it gives light to
all in the house. In the same way, let your light shine
before others, so that they may see your good works
and give glory to your Father who is in heaven.*

Matthew 5:14–16 ESV

W HEN I SAW THESE PLATES, they reminded me of my son, Jason, whom I miss more than I can possibly explain. Jason suffered from alcoholism for several years and was in and out of rehab several times. However, his death in December 2018 still came as a shock. I continue to have moments of feeling as though part of me is missing. But I knew this plate was a sign for me to remember that no matter what we go through on this earth, Jesus is with us. He carries us, and we should always glorify Him! He loves us and grieves with us. He also gives us peace even in those times of grief. Jesus, too, went through suffering, so He is able to help us through ours (Hebrews 2:18). He is all we need to fill in our missing pieces. Even in my grief, I want my life to glorify God.

Song: "We Will Glorify" by Twila Paris

Action Step: All of us experience deep grief and suffering, just as Jesus did. How does knowing that Jesus also suffered help comfort you?

_____

_____

_____

_____

_____

PRAYER

O God, may we glorify Your holy name,
for You are worthy! O God, give me the heart
to glorify You in all things.
Amen

GOD N LUV

Who is a God like you, who pardons sin and forgives
the transgression of the remnant of his inheritance?
You do not stay angry forever but delight to show
mercy.

Micah 7:18

GOD'S LOVE IS THE ONLY love that does not fail. God loves us because He created us and wants to see us grow. In fact, God *is* love.

Beloved, let us love one another, for love is from God, and whoever loves has been born of God and knows God. Anyone who does not love does not know God, because God is love. (1 John 4:7–8 ESV)

The characteristics of love are found in 1 Corinthians 13:4–81 (ESV):

Love is patient and kind; love does not envy or boast; it is not arrogant or rude. It does not insist on its own way; it is not irritable or resentful; it does not rejoice at wrongdoing, but rejoices with the truth. Love bears all things, believes all things, hopes all things, endures all things. Love never ends.

God is all of these things to us, and as Christ followers, as we pursue Him, these become true of us as well.

A lot of people do not realize that God does love us. *How can God love me?* they wonder. Talk to God, and renew your belief in Him. Remember, it is faith in God's love for you—not works to earn His love—so that no man can boast. As Micah 7:18 says, God *delights* to show mercy to us. Oh, what a loving, heavenly Father!

Song: "Love God Love People" by Danny Gokey

Action Step: Review the Scriptures above. Dwell on God's love for you and how these verses bring new understanding of God's love.

_____

_____

_____

_____

_____

PRAYER

Loving God, whether my day is good or difficult, let Your name be praised from my lips. Your love is an ocean, and it carries me through all my days.
Amen

HE HEALS

*I will praise God's name in song and glorify him
with thanksgiving.*

Psalm 69:30

I WENT TO A DOCTOR, AND he had a license plate in his office saying, HE HEALS. So many of us pray that doctors will be able to heal us and our loved ones. We also pray for strangers and acquaintances. We pray for those on prayer lists, and we pray on prayer teams, asking God to heal.

Healing does not necessarily mean a physical healing, as if we just had an operation or a procedure. Healing could be relational, after an altercation with a strong-willed child, or a misunderstanding with family or a friend. Healing could be from grief over losing a loved one or friend, or healing from a broken heart, anxiety, depression, and many other causes.

I love these verses about healing:

LORD my God, I called to you for help, and you healed me. (Psalm 30:2)

"But I will restore you to health and heal your wounds," declares the LORD. (Jeremiah 30:17)

I have been in need of both health and relationship healings. With my anxiety, I have felt healed at times only months later to have it come back. Some healings are instant; others either take time or don't happen. I pray daily for many things, including healing for me and others.

At times it feels like we are carrying our crosses for our Lord. Help me, Lord, to be able to carry it for You.

Song: "Healing Begins" by Tenth Avenue North

Action Step: Pour out your heart to God about an area that needs healing.

_____

_____

_____

_____

_____

PRAYER

Lord, You are our healer. You are able to do immeasurably more than all we ask or imagine according to Your power.
Amen

HECAN4U

"If you can?" said Jesus.
"Everything is possible for one who believes."

Mark 9:23

JESUS CAN FOR YOU, ACCORDING to His will. When we are in the valley or pit, drowning or grieving, in need of hope and healing, Jesus can for us.

I have prayed, pleaded, gotten on my knees, face to the ground, driven around listening to sermons and Christian music, and begged God to take my anxiety, but still I experience horrific anxiety. And yet, He works through the love of my family, friends, and loved ones. They have prayed for me and talked me through the feelings of anxiety that are so very hard to explain. Jesus can heal you in a second, a moment, a week, a month, a year, or years. We never know how, when, or if He will do what we ask, seek, knock, and pray for, but we do know He will do it according to His will.

Song: "Stand Up for Jesus" by Newsboys

Action Step: What is a prayer you have prayed where God didn't answer it the way you asked? How might He be answering it "according to His will" instead?

_____

_____

_____

_____

_____

PRAYER

Jesus, You are my helper. You live within me and tell me to ask and receive. Let me remember to ask for Your guidance and assistance when I feel unable. You will always make a way.
Amen

I B LEEV

*Then Jesus said to the centurion, "Go! Let it be done
just as you believed it would." And his servant was
healed at that moment.*

Matthew 8:13

*I*N THE PAST I HAVE seen plaques that say, "I BELIEVE," and over time, I find them to be a little cliché.

When my son graduated from elementary school, I decided to paint a picture of him standing outside the doors of his school with his arms up in the air and a caption that said, "Dreams do come true." I could not think of a better gift for his intervention specialist who always believed in my son, even when others did not. She not only believed that he would graduate from elementary school, but he would continue down this path of making a positive difference. She believed one day he would change the world.

This would not have been possible for my son without an intervention specialist who saw what others could not and stepped up to make a difference, took what we already knew, and made it happen.

Songs: "I Believe" by Geoff Moore and "I Gotta Believe" by Yolanda Adams

Action Step: What is a current struggle you have today where it's hard to believe? Name it, and each time you think about it, speak out loud the words of 1 John 5:14 (ESV): "And this is the confidence that we have toward him, that if we ask anything according to his will he hears us."

_____

_____

_____

_____

_____

PRAYER

O Lord, I believe! Help any unbelief in me be extinguished by the fire of Your love and Your faithfulness. Amen

MIRACLE

*Now Jesus performed many other miraculous
signs in the presence of the disciples, which are not
recorded in this book.*

John 20:30 (NET)

*M*Y OLD LICENSE PLATE WAS M H JESUS, "Miracles Happen
with Jesus." The apostle John wrote that Jesus performed
so many miracles that they could not ever be contained in
one book. When seeing my license plate, M H JESUS, people would
ask me, "What does the M H stand for?" In addition to, "Miracles
Happen with Jesus," I would ask what the M H meant to them, and
they would say "My Hero" or "My Healer" or "Most Holy."

One of my best friends has muscular dystrophy and has a
pacemaker, thyroid cancer, kidney cancer, and breast cancer. Her
pacemaker was put in incorrectly, and they had to move it when they
removed her breast.

When she realized something was wrong, she was sent directly to
a pacemaker specialist who told her to get her things in order because
there was no one in the United States who could do surgery on this
pacemaker that was put in incorrectly.

But God had other plans. Because of the cancer on one breast, she was able to have the pacemaker removed and a new one put in by a doctor at a Cleveland clinic. It was a medical miracle.

I know in my lifetime I have experienced small and big miracles, and I will never, on this side of heaven, be able to praise God enough.

Song: "Miracles" by Vertical Worship

Action Step: God is performing miracles all around us. Many times we miss them due to daily distractions. As you go through your day, look for big and small ways He is at work.

_____

_____

_____

_____

_____

PRAYER

Dearest Jesus, You say in Your Word that when You gave the disciples the Holy Spirit, they would do great things, even greater than You did on this earth. I pray You use us to perform many miracles in Your name.
Amen

SEEK H1M

You will seek me and find me
when you seek me with all your heart.

Jeremiah 29:13

ON THE WAY TO THE last moms college weekend where I went to visit my daughter, I saw the license plate, SEEK H1M. Later I saw DNT WRY as soon as I pulled into my daughter's driveway. All weekend long, Jesus was trying to tell me to SEEK HIM and NOT TO WORRY.

As a parent, at times that is a hard thing to do—the "do not worry" part. As a father, God loves our children more than we can imagine, and He is pursuing and loving our children even when they do not know it. The more I seek the Lord, the less I worry about my children. In my time with Him, He brings peace and confidence that they are in His hands. He reminds me that as much as I love my child, He loves them more.

Song: "Psalm 27 (One Thing)" by Shane & Shane

Action Step: Some of us have not known the love of good parents. Even in Psalm 27, the psalmist admits this in verse 10 (ESV): "For my father and my mother have forsaken me, but the LORD will take me in." As a parent, or as a child, how can you seek God more so that you will begin to love as He does?

_____

_____

_____

_____

_____

PRAYER

Father, I thank You for bringing me into Your flock. I pray for friends and family who are lost, that they would hear You quietly whispering into their hearts, "Jesus." For those who hear, let them seek You with all that they are.
Amen

MSTRPCE

*For we are God's masterpiece. He has created us
anew in Christ Jesus, so we can do the good things
he planned for us long ago.*

Ephesians 2:10 (NLT)

WE ARE GOD'S MASTERPIECE MADE in Christ Jesus. I really never thought of myself as a masterpiece, His greatest piece of work. It's amazing that we represent His best work, His creation!

Like a sculptor, He is constantly chipping away at the parts that need chipping in order for His perfect work to be transformed and made into His likeness. And as He sculpts, it can be painful! In these times, it's easy to be discouraged and believe that God is mad at us or we are being punished; rather, God is at work because He loves us! In order for us to do the good things He has planned for us, we must be transformed into the likeness of His Son, Jesus.

He has gifted each one of us with gifts that serve the body of Christ—whether it be teaching, evangelizing, serving, pastoring, giving, etc. And when we work together in unity, using our gifts to build up the body of Christ, then we are *truly* His masterpiece, His body!

Song: "Masterpiece" by Danny Gokey

Action Step: Do you know what one or two of your gifts are? If not, ask a close friend what you are good at that comes easy to you but not to others. That may give you a hint. To study more on gifts of the Spirit, you can read Ephesians 4, 1 Corinthians 12, 1 Peter 4:10–11, Romans 12:3–8. Write about what the body of Christ— God's masterpiece—could look like if we all played our part.

_____

_____

_____

_____

_____

PRAYER

Lord, we are Your masterpieces, and here is a verse that shows that—Ephesians 2:10: "For we are God's handiwork, created in Christ Jesus to do good works, which God prepared in advance for us to do." Help us to fulfill Your will for our lives!
Amen

I KNOW

"For I know the plans I have for you," declares the
LORD, *"plans to prosper you and not to harm you,*
plans to give you hope and a future."

Jeremiah 29:11

*T*HIS SCRIPTURE IS OFTEN FOUND on graduation cards and used to encourage those who are going through a hard time. What we need to remember is the context of this passage. The Israelites had been banished from their land because they weren't following God. For seventy years, they were exiled. During this season, the Lord promised that if they turned back to Him and sought Him wholeheartedly, He had plans for them, and they were good. The purpose of the exile was to turn them back to God, to repent, so He could bless them.

And the same is true for us. When we go through hard times, it's possible God is disciplining us (Hebrews 12:7–11) so we will turn back to Him and seek Him wholeheartedly. How can we see our hard times as hopeful, as God's way of pursuing us so He can bless us? Romans 5:3–5 (ESV) says:

Not only that, but we rejoice in our sufferings, knowing that suffering produces endurance, and endurance produces character, and character produces hope, and hope does not put us to shame, because God's love has been poured into our hearts through the Holy Spirit who has been given to us.

God *knows* His plans for us are good when we seek Him. When we know and believe this, we can go through suffering with hope.

Song: "I Know" by Big Daddy Weave

Action Step: What is a current situation that is painful? Might God be trying to get your attention? Take some time to sit with Him in prayer, asking Him to show you how to better seek Him, *knowing* what He knows—that His plans for you are good.

_____

_____

_____

_____

_____

PRAYER

Lord, from Your Word in Romans 15:29, "I know that when I come to You, I will come in the full measure of the blessing of Christ."
Amen

HES ABLE

*Now to him who is able to do immeasurably
more than all we ask or imagine, according to his
power that is at work within us, to him be glory
in the church and in Christ Jesus throughout all
generations, for ever and ever! Amen.*

Ephesians 3:20-21

GOD, JESUS, AND THE HOLY Spirit are able to love us, save us, help us, guide us, heal us, and do more than all we ask or imagine. Through Scripture, in the lives of those who walked with Him, we see this. And He does it for those of us who walk with Him now.

As we know God more and more through His Word and through prayer, we see His love for us and His power in our lives as we walk with Him in obedience. It is through us, His church, that He works in our world, and when we listen to His promptings, we will see Him do immeasurably more than we could ever imagine!

Song: "He's Able" by The Richard Smallwood Singers

Action Step: Is there something in your life God has given you a passion to do for Him? Perhaps it's to raise a family or pursue a career with the gifts He has given you. What is that thing deep in your heart God is calling you to do but you have struggled to believe He is able? Talk with Him about it. Ask Him to show you the way.

_____

_____

_____

_____

_____

PRAYER

Father, some days I don't feel up to the task. I am tired and complaining and feel what is in front of me is impossible. But You make all things possible. I pray for Your strength and energy to complete what I set out to do.
Amen

FAITH76 & FAITH73

And whatever you ask in prayer,
you will receive, if you have faith.

Matthew 21:22 (ESV)

SEEING FAITH76 AND FAITH73 REMINDED me of my husband, Don, and me. We graduated from high school in 1973 and 1976 respectively. We did not find out until we began dating in 1985, when I was twenty-seven and he was thirty, that we had attended the same high school. We had never met as we were three years apart, and our high school was tenth through twelfth grade. I had always had faith in God and Jesus, and had prayed to God to lead me to find the right person to spend my life with. God has fulfilled His promise to me, and Don and I have been married for thirty-five years (2022) and counting.

Song: "Walk by Faith" by Jeremy Camp

Action Step: What are you currently praying for that requires faith to believe?

_____

_____

_____

_____

_____

PRAYER

Jesus, I have faith in You. I believe You will complete the works You have started in me.

Amen

IAM4UJC

To him be glory in the church and in Christ Jesus
throughout all generations, for ever and ever! Amen.

Ephesians 3:21

*I*MET WITH A LONGTIME FRIEND for lunch, and she shared this license plate with me. It declares that we are for Jesus Christ and sharing Him with others. We are blessed to still be able to share our faith publicly in this country. I pray for people in countries where they cannot share their faith without consequence, but are at times threatened, jailed, and even martyred for their faith in Christ. They show us what it means to truly be *for* Christ when under attack, even giving their very lives. I am inspired by those whose faith is strengthened in conflict like this. I pray that if ever a time comes when sharing my faith is prohibited, I, too, will be strengthened to stand.

We believers are all united in God's kingdom around the world, a spiritual kingdom. In the end, if we stay faithful to Him, we will have our victory in Christ.

Song: "Who You Say I Am" by Hillsong Worship

Action Step: Is there someone in your life who needs to hear the good news of Jesus Christ? Who can you pray for and talk with about His great love for them?

_____

_____

_____

_____

_____

PRAYER

Lord, may others know I am for Jesus when I show Your love and follow Your ways.
Amen

JESUS N I

At that time Jesus said, "I praise you, Father, Lord of heaven and earth, because you have hidden these things from the wise and learned, and revealed them to little children."

Matthew 11:25

JESUS BLESSED ME WHEN I wasn't aware, almost ten years ago. I did not have a relationship with Jesus or God. I was a born-again believer who at times was a churchgoer and did lots of Bible studies. Some of these license plates remind me of my lack of relationship with God.

These past five years have been the hardest mentally in my entire life due to the anxiety I suffer. But it has been something God has used in my life to bring me closer to Him, to rely on Him and seek His comfort.

The image of Jesus with little children is a visual for us of how God sees us. We are His dearly loved children; He wants to share His heart with us and have a relationship with us! A loving Father with His child. I see Jesus and me together as He reveals His heart to me through prayer and through His Word. Saint Faustina wrote daily in her diary about her time with Jesus. I desire to have that kind of relationship with Him! Jesus I trust in You! Divine Mercy.

Song: "Jesus I Believe" by Big Daddy Weave

Action Step: How does the image of Jesus revealing hidden things to children inspire you in your relationship with Him?

_____

_____

_____

_____

_____

PRAYER

Jesus, You and I are able to be close and at peace. You take care of my heart and mind. I have a peaceful spirit when I pray to You and think of You.
Amen

MSGR 4 JC

Truly, truly, I say to you, a servant is not greater
than his master, nor is a messenger greater
than the one who sent him.

John 13:16 (ESV)

I HAVE SEEN THREE DIFFERENT LICENSE plates (MSSNGR1 MSSNGR2 MESSNGR) about being a messenger for Jesus Christ. My friend Vicki has seen two. With the Holy Spirit leading us, we both are messengers for Christ!

As I go about my days, at times I wonder, *Is God is prompting me to do something for Him?* Sometimes He prompts me to give a Divine Mercy bracelet to a stranger. Other times, it's through various license plates I strike up conversations with others about how good God is. I am always seeking ways to be His messenger, and I am grateful to serve Him in this way.

Isaiah 6:8 (ESV) says, "And I heard the voice of the Lord saying, 'Whom shall I send, and who will go for us?' Then I said, 'Here am I! Send me.'" Serving God is an honor and privilege. Let's be messengers for Him.

Song: "The Message" by 4Him

Action Step: "Here am I! Send me" is a bold prayer! Could you pray it? Why or why not?

_____

_____

_____

_____

_____

PRAYER

Your Word, O Lord, says, "How beautiful are the feet of those who bring good news."
Help us be Your messengers of hope to the lost, walking wherever You lead us.
Amen

SECTION 7

WAITING

WAIT 4 HM

*One thing I ask from the L*ORD*, this only do I seek:*
*that I may dwell in the house of the L*ORD *all the days*
*of my life, to gaze on the beauty of the L*ORD *and to*
seek him in his temple.

Psalm 27:4

GOD KNOWS HOW LONG I have been waiting to accomplish what He put on my heart. My story was a ministry with an innate sense that it needed to be shared and would help many others. But the struggles, doubt in myself, and tears were too many to count. So many false starts, changes in direction, and my own lack of faith in myself and in what I believed my purpose to be had me sidelined. Some cherished Scripture which lent encouragement to me are verses in Psalm 27 (1, 4–5, 13–14).

Seeing Psalm 27:14 in the back of a truck window was a message I profoundly held onto. It was accompanied by the written verse: "Wait for the LORD; be strong and take heart and wait for the Lord." God's timing is so certainly not our timing, and I pray to always have faith and wait, knowing God is with me.

Song: "Psalm 27" by Jonathan Ogden

Action Step: What is something you are waiting for?

_____

_____

_____

_____

_____

PRAYER

*Jesus, as I wait for You to heal my body,
mind, and spirit, I trust in You.
Amen*

W8 4 GOD

Wait for the Lord;
be strong and take heart and wait for the Lord.

Psalm 27:14

OD KNOWS I AM WAITING on Him to help me with many difficult things happening in my life, specifically this crippling anxiety I have suffered with. Each day, I seek Him, praying to be free of it.

In 2 Corinthians 12:7–10, Paul talks about the "thorn in flesh" that he pleaded with God to take away from him. But God told him, No. While we don't know what it was specifically, we know it was causing him pain. Instead of removing the thorn, God told Paul, "My grace is sufficient for you, for my power is made perfect in weakness" (2 Corinthians 12:9). It's when we are weak that God's strength can be revealed in us.

> But they who wait for the Lord shall renew their strength; they shall mount up with wings like eagles; they shall run and not be weary; they shall walk and not faint. (Isaiah 40:31 ESV)

As I wait for the Lord in the middle of my suffering, I take heart that in my weakness, God's strength will renew mine.

Songs: "Wait On The Lord" by Donnie McClurkin and "Wait on God" by Hezekiah Walker

Action Step: What "thorn in the flesh" do you need to talk with God about? How can you wait on the Lord as He renews your strength?

_____

_____

_____

_____

_____

PRAYER

Dearest God, I wait for Your words to warm my heart.
Help me to stay in Your Word, the Bible.
Waiting on You, God, is not always easy,
but with Your help and strength, I can do everything.
With God, all things are possible.
Amen

GOD IS GD

Oh give thanks to the Lord, for he is good,
for his steadfast love endures forever!

Psalm 107:1 ESV

OD IS GOOD ALL THE time, and all the time God is good! In March of 2014, my husband and I went to the theater to see the movie, *God's Not Dead.* We loved it! The preacher in the movie said, "God is good all the time, and all the time God is good." This license plate reminded me of that.

It can be hard to believe God is good *all the time.* When we experience something hard or painful, it's easy to believe God is punishing us or has forgotten about us. Rather, it can be God building our character and making us stronger. Throughout Scripture, we see God using hard times to lead people to Himself so they can experience His deep love for them.

Song: "God Is Good" by Hillsong Worship

Action Step: Are you going through a hard season? Or have you recently experienced something painful? How might God use that to reveal His goodness and deep love for you?

_____

_____

_____

_____

_____

<u>PRAYER</u>

God, I pray with You today to thank You for Your goodness, mercy, and grace. Even when I have been awful, You have shown me Your love again and again. Let me remember You in all I do and share good today with everyone in my path.

Amen

PSALM 40

I waited patiently for the LORD;
he turned to me and heard my cry.

Psalm 40:1

USUALLY WHEN I AM WAITING for someone, there is a limit to how long I do so patiently. Maybe I can wait patiently for an hour, as I have done when waiting for my kids to finish a college entrance exam, or maybe I can only last thirty seconds, like when I want to get going, *now!*

When something is promised to us and it is something very good, while we may wait excitedly, if we know it *will* happen, then we can usually wait with a decent amount of calm. What would our wait look like if it was a wait of absolute faith in the outcome? Jesus wants us to wait for Him just like that—in full and complete faith that we know the outcome. The end of the story is clear. When we need to cry out to Jesus, we should do so in faith that He hears our cry, that He sees us waiting, and that both of us are grounded in His promises.

Song: "Psalm 40" by NewSong

Action Step: Is waiting hard for you? During the waiting, take time to praise and worship Him and see how it changes your heart and your perspective.

_____

_____

_____

_____

_____

PRAYER

Dear Lord, thank You for hearing me when I cry out to You. Help me to stand strong and expectantly as I wait, praising Your name always.
Amen

NVR GV UP

Therefore, since we are surrounded by such a great cloud of witnesses, let us throw off everything that hinders and the sin that so easily entangles. And let us run with perseverance the race marked out for us, fixing our eyes on Jesus, the pioneer and perfecter of faith.

Hebrews 12:1-2

PANDEMIC, LOCKDOWNS, POLITICAL UNREST, WARS, and human tragedy. Family disputes and church hurt. Daily hardships and personal trials. We can feel overwhelmed and exhausted by all that we face. How do we keep going and never give up?

Take time to read Hebrews 11 and hear the stories of those who have gone before us. Sometimes when we can see that we are not alone, that others have gone through hard things and have persevered, it can revive our hope to continue on.

When Peter wanted to walk on water, out to where Jesus was, he started to sink when he took his eyes off of Jesus and put them on the waves (Matthew 14:22–33). When we shift our focus to our problem instead of the Perfector of our faith, we, too, will lose faith! We must shift our focus back to our Perfector and keep our eyes on Him. He is the only one who can help us persevere and never give up.

Songs: "Never Give Up" by Yolanda Adams and "I Believe" by Geoff Moore

Action Step: What problem are you currently facing that makes you want to give up? Ask God to help you keep your eyes on Him, to persevere, and give you fresh perspective and hope to keep going!

_____

_____

_____

_____

_____

PRAYER

Holy Spirit, I will never give up on You, God, and Jesus—blessed Trinity. Even when the feelings and thoughts of giving up come to me, I will stop and pray and move forward.
Amen

BE STILL

Be still and know that I am God.

Psalm 46:10

SOME OF US EXPERIENCE MORE anxiety the older we get. Mine has been crippling, keeping me on the couch off and on for many months. Life can be funny at times, and how interesting that it was my anxiety that forced me to stop and be still.

In our culture, things move fast and furious. Social media and the internet give us instant access to information, people, and material things we need. It's hard to wait when we don't have to. But our instant society has not made us more content, just more restless.

What does it look like to be still and know that He is God?

When a mama dog wants to bring one of her puppies back to her, she will pick it up with her mouth by the scruff. As soon as she grabs that restless puppy, he instantly relaxes into his mama's grip because he trusts her completely. That's the image of being still before God. To relax into Him, fully trusting that He has us in His grip.

As we read all of Psalm 46, it says that nations are in uproar and kingdoms fall. That things are in chaos. BUT GOD. HE is our refuge and strength! An ever-present help in trouble. That even when the earth gives way, the mountains fall into the sea, the waters roar and foam, and the mountains quake with their surging, God's got this. And He's got us. He is our fortress where we can hide and be safe.

What if in our most anxious times we could shift our focus to that image of being in God's grip, fully trusting Him to carry us through the chaos, and cover us with His peace and protection?

Song: "Still (I Will Be Still)" by Juanita Bynum

Action Step: Close your eyes, take some deep breaths, and visualize yourself in God's loving grip, protecting you from the chaos. Praise Him for His strength and power; thank Him for holding you close and keeping you safe in the storm.

_____

_____

_____

_____

_____

PRAYER

Father God, I am thankful that I can be still. In the stillness, please continue to show me Your truths.
Amen

SECTION 8

PEACE

PCE 4 EVR

I will make a covenant of peace with them; it will be
an everlasting covenant. I will establish them and
increase their numbers, and I will put my sanctuary
among them forever.

Ezekiel 37:26

I WAS DRIVING AROUND TOWN ONE day, listening to a Chuck Swindoll message. As they talked about God's peace, I prayed for that peace. I was going to a women's Christian event that weekend and felt a little anxious, with a headache. As I prayed, I saw a license plate in front of me: PCE 4 EVR. I thanked God for always affirming and confirming His love to me.

The lyrics from Hillsong Young & Free's song, "Peace," remind me that God's peace is the only peace that calms my heart.

Song: "Peace" by Hillsong Young & Free

Action Step: Is there a song that brings God's peace to your heart when you hear it? The next time you find yourself anxious, dwell on God's peace and worship Him through that song.

PRAYER

*O Lord, You are our peace. May we be peace to others as
we demonstrate Your love, which will not let us go.*

Amen

B N JESUS

*So in Christ Jesus you are all children of God
through faith.*

Galatians 3:26

WHILE I WAS DRIVING TO Kitty's house for a visit, I saw the plate B N JESUS. Galatians 3:26–28 says:

So in Christ Jesus you are all children of God through faith, for all of you who were baptized into Christ have clothed yourselves with Christ. There is neither Jew nor Gentile, neither slave nor free, nor is there male and female, for you are all one in Christ Jesus.

I am grateful God came and invited us all into His family through Christ. In a world of isolation and rejection, how amazing to belong to the family of God. To be His children. Christ fulfilled the law for us so we could be free from the bondage of sin and death. So we could be in the eternal family of God. That is the good news of the gospel. We belong and we are accepted as we are—imperfect—because Christ transforms us into His likeness as we know Him better.

Song: "I Believe in Jesus" by Keith Matten

Action Step: Is it hard to believe that you don't have to do anything to earn God's love? That we just have to believe that Jesus is God's Son? What is the hardest part of believing this?

_____

_____

_____

_____

_____

PRAYER

Jesus, You give us peace, peace in our hearts and minds. We will have peace forever when we arrive in heaven and live with You, dearest Jesus, forever and ever and ever.
Amen

PEACE 4 U

Peace I leave with you; my peace I give you. I do not give to you as the world gives. Do not let your hearts be troubled and do not be afraid.

John 14:27

A FEW YEARS BACK, I SAW this plate. I remember a time that I thought I had peace, but really, I didn't. I visited with a friend, and she told me that her kids were all in a good place, she had moved into her dream home, and things were well. She said she was finally at peace.

What peace means to me is trusting God in all things. That through our trials and tribulations we can trust God will be there to listen and to help. I believe peace is not having fear, because fear is not from God. We are not given a spirit of fear. Peace is to surrender and give it to God. Jesus, I trust in You!

Song: "Pray for Peace" by Reba McEntire

Action Step: Name something you need to turn over to God and receive His peace.

_____

_____

_____

_____

_____

PRAYER

Lord, You are our peace. We pray You will keep our mind stayed on You as we trust You to keep us in perfect peace without fear.
Amen

DNT PANC

*Don't panic. I'm with you. There's no need to fear for
I'm your God. I'll give you strength. I'll help you. I'll
hold you steady, keep a firm grip on you.*

Isaiah 41:10 The Message

*I*WAS DRIVING HOME FROM A friend's house and saw a license plate, DNT PANC (Don't Panic). I had been dealing off and on with horrific anxiety. I spent a lot of time on the couch crying and praying to God for this to go away.

A short time later, I was in another state, and I was waiting in my car for my daughter. In that moment, I received a *Godwink* as I looked and saw one single car with the same plate: DNT PANC. When my daughter got into my car with our lunch, she asked why it looked like I was starting to cry. I told her about seeing the same plates in different states and that God and Jesus wanted me to know not to panic.

Song: "Don't Worry, Don't Panic" by Jon Bonner

Action Step: If you've ever panicked, what was it that helped you calm down? Many times, it's realizing we are safe, but sometimes our bodies panic against our will! The next time you are panicked, how can you lean more into the truth of Isaiah 41:10?

_____

_____

_____

_____

_____

PRAYER

Dearest Lord, we are blessed by Your messages and moments, exact moments when You show Yourself to us in all different ways. I saw "DNTPANC" in two different states within a short time, and You know I needed to see that. Thank You for Your watchful care.
Amen

GODS MOR

*Now to him who is able to do immeasurably more
than all we ask or imagine, according to his power
that is at work within us.*

Ephesians 3:20

OD IS MORE, AND HE does more than we can imagine. God has meant more to me these past many years than all the other years of my life. This is because I knew God back then, but I did not *really* know Him.

Over these past ten years, I have been in His Word, getting to know God more and more. During COVID-19, I was in three Zoom Bible studies! As I study and get to know Him, He reveals Himself to me.

God has shown me so much personal loving-kindness throughout my life, and I just did not at times see nor feel it because I wasn't in His Word, learning from and listening to Him. Since losing my brother Jerry, I feel God and His perfect ways. God is more!

Song: "Love Unrestrained" by Calvary

Action Step: Are you in the Word, reading and studying so you can know God more? If not, why do you suppose you don't spend time with God in this way? He has so much to tell us!

_____

_____

_____

_____

_____

PRAYER

Dear God, we know that You are more than everything in this world. We love You and thank You for always giving us more of You.
Amen

HE KNOWS

*But he knows the way that I take; when he has tested
me, I will come forth as gold.*

Job 23:10

Y FRIEND CATHY TEXTED ME that she had seen a license
plate, HE KNOWS. What she did not know was that it is
the name of one of my books: *He Knows. He Knows* is
about my life, my family's lives, both growing up and my immediate
family.

Soon after I saw the plate, my heart was heavy over some people
talking about God and how everyone gets to heaven. Even some of
the believers I know no longer feel Jesus is the only way to heaven.
But Jesus is the only way! In John 14:6, Jesus says, "I am the way and
the truth and the life. No one comes to the Father except through
me." And John 3:16 says, "For God so loved the world that he gave
his one and only Son, that whoever believes in him shall not perish
but have eternal life." It is *only* through Jesus that we can be saved and
go to heaven.

We are known and loved by God. He knows we are human and that we sin. I am thankful for such a God who loves us and is merciful. It's because He loves us so much that He saves us if we are willing to believe. I believe God, Jesus, and the Holy Spirit never ever give up on us, to save us, and they will try to get our attention even in the last moments of our life.

Songs: "He Knows" by Jeremy Camp and "He Knows" by Dan Bremnes

Action Step: You are fully known by God. How does that change your perspective, or how does it make you feel to be fully known and fully loved by the God of the universe?

_____

_____

_____

_____

_____

PRAYER

Dear Father God, I know that You know that I believe in You and Jesus and have the Holy Spirit living inside me. I appreciate the beauty You bring to my life.
Amen

NOT GOD

Listen, my dear brothers and sisters: Has not God chosen those who are poor in the eyes of the world to be rich in faith and to inherit the kingdom he promised those who love him?

James 2:5

"GOD, I'M NOT GOD: YOU ARE GOD" became my mantra during the second year of my recovery in the program of Alcoholics Anonymous. I still repeat it often. I had never heard the phrase "Not God." Yet many people around me and many of my readings suggested I had to stop playing God, especially if I wanted relief from the continuous stream of thoughts that would enter my mind. Not until I admitted, believed, and accepted that I was "Not God" was I given the relief I sought. It helped to read a book called, *Not God: A History of Alcoholics Anonymous*, by Ernest Kurtz.

In my attempt to control my own life and play God, I failed miserably. But when I learned to give my life over to Him—for Him to lead me and show me the way—I finally found peace. It can be scary to let go of control and see what God has. What if we don't like it? What if my life gets worse? I discovered God is faithful and only when we let Him lead can we truly find the abundant life He has for us.

Song: "There Is No God But God" by Elvis Presley

Action Step: Is there any area of your life that you are having a hard time letting go of control? What are you afraid of?

_____

_____

_____

_____

_____

PRAYER

Dear Abba God, we know that nothing happens in our lives unless You allow it. This can be the good, bad, and ugly. But You do allow things in our lives to grow us with our journey.
Amen

PHLP 4 67

Do not be anxious about anything, but in every situation, by prayer and petition, with thanksgiving, present your requests to God. And the peace of God, which transcends all understanding, will guard your hearts and your minds in Christ Jesus.

Philippians 4:6-7

*O*N FEBRUARY 16, 2016, I had not been able to sleep, afraid I was having a heart attack. I prayed silently for hours the verse mentioned above. I'd never had a panic attack before. Many of my loved ones struggle with anxiety, depression, bipolar, and PTSD. It is memorized verses I have for such times.

I knew my husband was exhausted, and I was going to pray through this to God and Jesus and the Holy Spirit. So I kept praying and praying. I prayed for hours, putting myself in the positions of others—those who are suffering, worldwide. I prayed all night—yes all night—without ceasing. And then a peace came over me and my entire body, a peace that surpasses all understanding. All of the pain I felt was gone.

I then started praying 1 Peter 5:7, paraphrasing the words: *Cast all your cares, burdens, sorrows, stress, busyness, anxiety, depression, worries, all your concerns, troubles, once and for all on Him, for He cares for you affectionately and cares about you watchfully. He is always thinking about you and watching everything that concerns you.*

When we take the time to earnestly pray, focusing on God's power instead of our problem, it changes our perspective, giving Him permission to bring us His peace.

Songs: "Do Not Be Anxious" by Seeds Family Worship and "Cast All Your Cares" by Beverley Knight

Action Step: What Scriptures can you pray and focus on today, inviting God's presence to bring you peace?

———————————————————————————

———————————————————————————

———————————————————————————

———————————————————————————

———————————————————————————

PRAYER

Heavenly Father, we give our anxieties to You with thanksgiving. Please give us Your peace that transcends all understanding as we lay down our requests and burdens to You.
Amen

BE WELL

He sent out his word and healed them;
he rescued them from the grave.

Psalm 107:20

*I*N THE SPRING OF 2016, Kitty and I were on our way to a Bible study. As we rode along, we talked about how God works in our lives, sometimes in mysterious ways. The subject was directed at Kitty. I was driving because the meds she was taking for her health issues made her unable to drive. We started looking for a parking place, and as soon as we found one, we looked over at the car beside us, and on the license plate it read, BE WELL.

I think we both looked at each other at the same time. This has to be through God! I feel that God connects with us through His loving, mysterious ways. Sometimes God brings physical healing to our bodies; sometimes it's spiritual. What we know is, having faith that He will heal us, however He chooses, can bring us peace and comfort.

God doesn't have to give us signs to comfort and bring us peace, but it sure is nice when He chooses to do so. He loves us, more than our minds can comprehend.

Songs: "It Is Well With My Soul" by Horatio Spafford and performed by Wintley Phipps and "It Is Well" by Kristene DiMarco

Action Step: Is there something you have been praying about for a long time, waiting on God to answer? Maybe it's a health concern where you are asking Him to make you well. Never give up praying. How can you be open to God's answer being different from your expectation of what it means to "be well"? Listen for His voice.

_____

_____

_____

_____

_____

PRAYER

Holy Spirit, bless You for blessing me by prompting me that I will be well. Please continue working in my life. Amen

SECTION 9

BLESSINGS

M BLEST

In a loud voice she exclaimed:
"Blessed are you among women,
and blessed is the child you will bear!"

Luke 1:42

*T*HERE ARE SO MANY DIFFERENT BLESSED and BLESS plates talking about how blessed we are. So many license plates show us just that. Yes, even though I am still carrying a cross, and it is so hard, God, Jesus, and the Holy Spirit help and enable me to carry it. There are days and nights when I wonder if I will make it. The anxiety and nervousness are so very painful. I have experienced myself the dark night of the soul.

Yesterday I saw M BLEST and M BLESSD in one day. So many affirmations. Jesus lets me see similar or the same license plates with different letters or numbers. The timing of seeing these plates in front of me is uncanny—the message is so clear.

So in the dark of the night as I struggle, I remember I am blessed and recount those blessings. This brings me to a new day. Thank You, Lord!

Song: "Bless the Broken Road" by Rascal Flatts

Action Step: Keep your eyes open for God's blessings, and count them!

_____

_____

_____

_____

_____

PRAYER

Dear Lord, help me to remember Your grace each day. Let me start each day with thanks to You and by counting my blessings and praising Your glory for each one. Amen

CHERISH

Cherish her, and she will exalt you;
embrace her, and she will honor you.

Proverbs 4:8

*I*CHERISH MY FAMILY, MY LOVED ones. I love them all with my whole heart, soul, and mind. The word *cherish* means protect and care for lovingly, to hold something dear.

In addition to my family and loved ones, I cherish our world and pray daily many times, now and for all future generations for salvation in Jesus, and for all healing and needs.

My time with my beloved brother Jerry is something I hold dear to my heart and cherish. Even when Jerry was with me here on earth, I cherished our sibling relationship. He was my best friend. When I can separate what wasn't great for him in this life and remember the purity of our time together, I have cherished memories of Jerry that I will carry with me until we meet again in the presence of Jesus.

Song: "Cherish the Love" by the Katinas

Action Step: In Proverbs 4:8, the author tells us to cherish wisdom because she will honor you. Wisdom brings us life! Take time to read chapter 4 of Proverbs to better understand why we need to cherish wisdom.

_____

_____

_____

_____

_____

PRAYER

Heavenly Father God, You cherish us all, Your children. You even tell us to become like children when we come to You. We, in turn, cherish and love You, Father.
Amen

D MERCY

Let Israel say: "His steadfast loves endures forever."
Let the house of Aaron say: "His steadfast love
endures forever." Let those who fear the LORD say:
"His steadfast love endures forever."

Psalms 118:2-4

GOD BROUGHT A FRIEND INTO my life at just the right time in a doctor's office I worked at. This demonstrated God's divine mercy through meeting Kitty, who is now one of my best friends.

I overheard her talking about God in the waiting room and later asked her about prayer. Kitty prayed for me out loud, and I told her that I do not recall ever being prayed for like that. Through the years, we have been there for each other for prayers for our families and loved ones, and we pray and ask for each other's prayer concerns all the time. We can depend on each other through the trials of life and through happy times. We get together now as married couples.

Divine mercy brought Kitty and me together in that office where we shared stories and prayed together about a situation that was on my mind. I would never have seen these license plates that she saw and told me about if it had not been for meeting her and becoming dear friends. How awesome is God's grace and mercy!

Song: "The Chaplet of Divine Mercy in Song" by St. Faustina and performed by Donna Cori Gibson

Action Step: Be looking for God today through interactions with others. Are there people you can talk with that need to be encouraged? Or perhaps there is someone who can encourage you today, if only you take the time to interact.

_____

_____

_____

_____

_____

PRAYER

Dearest Jesus, we are so thankful You want a relationship with us! Help us to grow closer to You every day.
Amen

DGOD4US

His divine power has given us everything we need for a godly life through our knowledge of him who called us by his own glory and goodness.

2 Peter 1:3

*W*E SAW THIS LICENSE PLATE on a vehicle. We were not sure what the D stood for but thought it meant *divine.* I know that God is for us at all times. God is divine. Sometimes we may have a hard time making a decision, but God is with us. He is rooting for us. God is for us at all times. Never changing. Praise be to God.

During my long period of illness, when many times I felt like giving up, God showed up for me so personally that I was sure He had His hand on me for a brighter future. I read 2 Peter 1:3 about God's divine power and how His divine power gives us all we need, at all times.

His divine power has given us everything we need for a godly life through our knowledge of Him who called us by his own glory and goodness, confirming one's calling and election.

Song: "Divine Romance" by Phil Wickham

Action Step: Is there a situation you are facing today that requires God's divine power? Pray and ask God to give you all you need to handle the situation.

_____

_____

_____

_____

_____

PRAYER

Jesus, we thank You for Your divine mercy. God, You are divine and full of power and glory and so gracious to us all. Amen

WRITE

Then the LORD said to Moses, "Write down these words, for in accordance with these words I have made a covenant with you and with Israel."

Exodus 34:27

*I*EXPLAINED TO THE OWNER OF the vehicle of this plate about my book and that I had wanted to write a story about my brothers and my life. This never came to fruition as I had a tendency to procrastinate. She said her husband is the published author of over forty books. I told her about the books Jesus/God put on my heart nine years ago after my brother passed away, and that friends and I have now seen over nine hundred and fifty Christian and positive plates.

I have many friends who recently said they felt compelled to help me write my license-plate stories. I feel that through writing this book, I am telling my story and the stories of others touched by Jesus.

In the song "Write Your Story," Francesca Battistelli asks God to write *His* story on her heart. What I love about God is how His story weaves through ours, and when we tell our story and what He has done in our lives, we are telling His story too, and we are sharing His amazing love with others.

Second Corinthians 3:2–3 says, "You yourselves are our letter, written on our hearts, known and read by everyone. You show that you are a letter from Christ, the result of our ministry, written not with ink but with the Spirit of the living God, not on tablets of stone but on tablets of human hearts."

When we share our story and God's story, we are writing it on human hearts. It is no longer temporary. It is an eternal message of God's love.

Song: "Write Your Story" by Francesca Battistelli

Action Step: How can you better tell the story of God with the story of your life?

_____

_____

_____

_____

_____

PRAYER

God, Jesus, bless You for all the writings in the Old and New Testaments—so many writers that the Holy Spirit helped to write the Bible.
Amen

FAVOGOD

In him we were also chosen, having been predestined
according to the plan of him who works out
everything in conformity with the purpose of his will.

Ephesians 1:11

ECAUSE GOD CREATED EACH AND every one of us, we are each a favorite of God. It is hard for humans to comprehend this for several reasons. Maybe you grew up not feeling favored or valued. Maybe the choices you have made have not been wise. Some walk with a sense of past "baggage" or guilt and think, *I cannot be a favorite of God's.* Maybe we were raised to be too humble. But you are favored.

If you need to make it right with God, go to Him in private and tell Him everything. Psalm 84:11 says: "For the LORD God is a sun and shield; the LORD bestows favor and honor; no good thing does God withhold from those whose walk is blameless."

We are not favored because of something we've done, but simply because we are God's children. Parents talk about this love they have for their child they cannot comprehend. Nothing the child does stops that parent from loving their child. They love them simply because they are theirs.

God loves us deeply simply because we are His children.

Song: "I Am Favored" by Tomi Favored

Action Step: How can you lean into the favor of God today? Know that you are completely and fully loved and favored by Him, simply because you are His.

_____

_____

_____

_____

_____

PRAYER

God, we are forever grateful for Your favor for us. We are so highly favored. Bless You, God. Amen

GDSGOOD

Surely God is good to Israel,
to those who are pure in heart.

Psalm 73:1

ADEAR FRIEND OF MINE, KATHY B., texted me a picture of the plate GOD'S GOOD. Many of my friends have seen this license plate in different states. I started singing the song when I saw the plate.

God is so good, God is so good,
God is so good, He's so good to me!

God has been so good to me. I know His whole book, the Bible, repeats that message. And the gospel of Jesus is good news! I know He is with me, even as I struggle with some anxiety issues. He knows us, He loves us, and He is for us. God's good.

For me, when I see this license plate, I am reminded of my caring husband, my beautiful daughters, my family and friends, and my path to Christ. My early life was not always easy, but God never left me, and He did not forget to give easy things to me also. For all this and more, I am thankful to see God's goodness.

In Psalm 73, the psalmist starts off by saying God is good. He had his doubts! He was envious of the prosperity of the wicked men around him. Why were they seemingly blessed with good things, while the righteous seemed to be punished with suffering? But as he pondered the truth, he knew that his life and salvation were wrapped in the goodness of God. The joy of the Lord was his strength! In the end, the wicked would be destroyed, but he would be with God.

God is good! The good news is that Jesus took our sin so we could be free from it, free to walk with God right into eternity.

Song: "God Is Good All the Time" by Don Moen

Action Step: Do you sometimes get discouraged when you see evil men prosper but godly men suffer? Read through Psalm 73 and be encouraged that God is good!

PRAYER

God, I thank You for Your goodness, mercy, and grace. Even when I have been awful, You have shown me Your love again and again. Let me remember You in all I do, and share good today with everyone in my path.

Amen

JC IS KNG

*That he worked in Christ when he raised him from the
dead and seated him at his right hand in the heavenly
places, far above all rule and authority and power and
dominion, and above every name that is named, not
only in this age but also in the one to come.*

Ephesians 1:20-21 ESV

KITTY SHARED WITH ME HER prayers in wanting to see a license plate during our visit together for our girls' weekend. On our way to her house we saw "JC IS KNG" (Jesus Christ is King). So often these girls' weekends become a respite, a way to unplug from our day-to-day lives and to reconnect with really great friends. Kitty is this for me.

My life can be rather hectic at times but also very rewarding. I have a son with autism, and while the worry can be all-consuming, my son has made me a better person. Seeing JC IS KNG affirmed for me that I am not in control; God is, and everything is going to be okay. This was a comforting feeling as we continued on our way to Kitty's house. We were both in the right place at the right time, His time.

Song: "Go Tell It on the Mountain" by Zach Williams

Action Step: Who needs to hear your story of how Jesus became your king of your life?

_____

_____

_____

_____

_____

PRAYER

Jesus, You are King of kings, Lord of lords.
May we live our lives submitted to Your authority
as Your faithful children.
Amen

GIV IT AWY

You will be enriched in every way so that you can be generous on every occasion, and through us your generosity will result in thanksgiving to God.

2 Corinthians 9:11

*W*HEN I FIRST SAW THIS plate I thought it meant to give it to God. Giving to God can mean giving generously to others, being His hands and feet in the world, providing for those around us in need. God uses us to bring blessing on our neighbors.

We experience great joy when we give to others. My goal is to be a blessing to someone each day. Sometimes this looks like giving in faith, giving more than we have. In 2 Corinthians 9, the apostle Paul talks to the believers about giving and that as they gave, God would continue to give to them, so they would always have enough. I want my faith to be strong enough that I, too, can give generously to others, trusting God's promise to supply for my needs as I supply for the needs of others.

One way I give is through my ministry. I purchase bracelets in bulk from a Christian store in Bosnia, and then I strike up conversations with strangers and many times gift them with these beautiful bracelets. I do have the gift of gab, and I give it away! But giving can also be with your time and your resources that you have. Giving is a sure way to forget your own troubles.

I have found joy in just simple things like taking a meal to someone who has had surgery, sending a card of encouragement, praying with someone, and listening to hurting people.

My giving it away just involves mostly time but touches lives and demonstrates God's love and generosity.

Song: "Generous Giver" by Vintage Worship

Action Step: Read 2 Corinthians 9:1–15. What do you learn about giving, and how can you apply it to your life?

_____

_____

_____

_____

_____

PRAYER

All we have is from You, Lord. May we freely give away to those in need. Help us see the need and meet it by Your glorious riches.
Amen

GIV THKS

Give thanks in all circumstances; for this is God's will for you in Christ Jesus.

1 Thessalonians 5:18

SEEING THIS LICENSE PLATE REMINDED me of a song by singer Don Moen titled "Give Thanks."

I heard the song for the first time at a funeral home. It was being played for a woman—a mom and wife—who had taken her life. As I cried at the lyrics and at the family's loss, I also cried for the loss of my brother, who had also taken his life. I gave thanks for having a brother like Jerry, the kindest most loving best brother ever. Though Jerry was younger than me, he was my protector from a young age, making sure to escort me to my friends to get to school in the dark early mornings. As adults, Jerry was my confidant and listening ear. He was a kind and compassionate brother who was a true friend. All that knew him loved him.

At times it is hard to give thanks for hard, difficult, sorrowful situations, but when you know that your loved one is for sure with God and Jesus, it gives you joy. Your hope is in being together in heaven. Let us give thanks for all that God, Jesus, and the Holy Spirit have given us.

Song: "Give Thanks" by Don Moen

Action Step: As you consider a difficult situation in your life, name three things you can give thanks for in the middle of it.

_____

_____

_____

_____

_____

PRAYER

O Lord, we give thanks to You, for You are good, and Your loving devotion endures forever. Help us give thanks in all circumstances, because You are always with us and working everything together for good for those who love You and are called to Your purposes.

Amen

JESU JOY

At that time Jesus, full of joy through the Holy Spirit, said, "I praise you, Father, Lord of heaven and earth, because you have hidden these things from the wise and learned, and revealed them to little children. Yes, Father, for this is what you were pleased to do."

Luke 10:21

HAVING A RELATIONSHIP WITH JESUS brings me joy. In the trials, tribulations, and dark nights of the soul, Jesus is with us, which comforts me. He, too, has suffered, and knows what we feel. The apostle Paul tells us we find joy in our trials because it develops perseverance, strengthens our faith, and matures us. Trials are not a joy to go through, but they produce joy.

Jesus is with us when a baby brings joy coming into this world. Joy is with us at a wedding or in a relationship. Joy is with us when we pray for and help one another. Joy comes in the morning.

Song: "Jesu, Joy of Man's Desiring" by Josh Groban

Action Step: Think about a trial you have gone through and how it made you stronger. Can you see the joy it produced? If not, pray and ask God to show you joy.

_____

_____

_____

_____

_____

PRAYER

You have filled us with an inexpressible and glorious joy, for we are receiving the end result of our faith, the salvation of our souls. Thank You, Jesus!
Amen!

GODTHXU

Keep yourselves in God's love as you wait
for the mercy of our Lord Jesus Christ
to bring you to eternal life.

Jude 1:21

OD'S LOVE IS UNCONDITIONAL. WHAT an incredible gift God has bestowed upon us. A love that will not be denied, even when we fail and succumb to sinful ways. As long as we repent for our sins, God forgives us.

God, thank You for loving Your believers so much that You were willing to send Your only begotten Son to be among us. God, thank You for Your Son, who because of His love for the believers, took on death on the cross to take away the sins of our flesh. Jesus's death on the cross opened the way for all faithful followers of His to be able to enjoy the reward of life eternal in the kingdom of heaven. What an incredible gift! By living a God-centered life, we are given the opportunity to join God in His kingdom for eternity. We will be blessed to gather with all the other people whose lives were lived in accordance with the Ten Commandments, and have also been blessed with the ultimate reward of life forever in heaven.

God, thank You!

Song: "Dig a Little Deeper" by Mahalia Jackson

Action Step: Do you have a gratitude list? Today, write down what you are thankful for.

_____

_____

_____

_____

_____

PRAYER

God, You have an enormous heart, and You love us, and when we do Your will, we know that makes You happy. Amen

GD WINKS

I will instruct you and teach you in the way you should go; I will counsel you with my loving eye on you.

Psalm 32:8

*G*ODWINKS ARE SIGNS FROM GOD, who is interested in everything we do and shows us His presence in our everyday lives. We often think things that happen to us are coincidences when they are actually gifts from a loving God.

I had a best friend from high school whom I lost touch with, and I prayed someday our paths would cross again. She taught me about Christianity, and that was new to me because my family did not go to church. Years later, I started searching for more answers and eventually became a Christian. I really wanted to share my journey with her, since she had opened that door. My husband was in the air force, so we moved several times, and I finally gave up the idea of ever seeing her again.

One day my sister called and said she had a surprise for me . . . her new neighbor was my friend's sister, and she had been trying to connect with me also. We set a date, and I visited her only to find she had cancer and was not expected to live much longer. She had prayed for me for twenty-three years!

We spent the most wonderful three days together in September before she passed away in December. God filled that ache in my heart, and I will always be grateful. Kitty talked so highly about Squire Rushnell's *Godwink* book series, and I have them now too. I'm enjoying each book.

Song: "Somewhere Over the Rainbow" by Israel Kamakawiwo'ole

Action Step: Have you ever experienced a *Godwink?* How can *Godwinks* strengthen our faith?

_____

_____

_____

_____

_____

PRAYER

Lord, when we seek Your kingdom,
You give us the desires of our hearts.
Amen

GODGAVE

For God so loved the world that he gave his one and only Son, that whoever believes in him shall not perish but have eternal life.

John 3:16

GOD GAVE ME MY LOVING husband, Don, and our two precious daughters, who are the most loving, compassionate, beautiful women. My father-in-law once told me, "Kitty, these are not your daughters. They are God's, and He is gifting them to you. They are His."

Don and I raised them, and I am forever grateful for God giving me my family. I believe we end up with people coming and going in our lives and making a difference, and because God loves us, we are here to help one another and to be like Christ.

It's because of God's greatest gift—His Son Jesus—that we can love those around us in various ways: kind words, acts of service, praying for them. God's love for us motivates us to love others. Sharing God's love is the greatest gift we can give others.

Song: "God Gave Me A Song" by Oslo Gospel Choir

Action Step: Ask God who you can share His love with today. What is one tangible thing you can do? Maybe it's taking dinner to a neighbor who is sick, calling a friend who is hurting, or having an encouraging conversation with the cashier at the store.

_____

_____

_____

_____

PRAYER

Father, You are the giver of life. You gave Your one and only Son so that those who believe in Him will have life everlasting. Thank You for the gift of Jesus.
Amen

GD GOT US

For the Son of Man came to seek
and to save the lost.

Luke 19:10

Y HUSBAND AND I WERE lifelong believers in God, and we had attended the church of my youth, but we were not following Jesus. Through many marital struggles and false starts, we had finally settled into a new church home after attending the baptism of our dear friend Kitty with our four children.

While we had believed in God and the church and all that was holy, it wasn't until we came to this particular church that I was overcome by a new feeling and awakening of the presence of Jesus. I was changing, and while I had always believed, attended church, and looked for God, now I had found the missing pieces and decided I had been born new into a life with Christ. Now how was I going to tell my husband? But I needn't worry because the exact same thing was happening to him at the exact same time! What a gift we had been given!

Two years later, we were attending college orientation with our daughter and had left her to go grab something to eat. Walking through the parking lot, we turned for our vehicle, and directly in our path was our validation on a car license plate: GD GOT US. Indeed, He did.

Song: "First Love" by Chris Tomlin

Action Step: How has God spoken to you in a delightful way that was unexpected? Look for Him to speak to you as you go about your day.

_____

_____

_____

_____

_____

PRAYER

Lord, how we love You.
Thank You for loving us first and for calling us by name.
We pray for any seeking you and those who are lost,
that they would step into Your joy and light.
Amen

GD GOT US

Dear Lord Jesus, I know that I am a sinner, and I ask for Your forgiveness. I believe You died for my sins and rose from the dead. I turn from my sins and invite You to come into my heart and life. I want to trust and follow You as my Lord and Savior. In Your Name. Amen.

ACKNOWLEDGMENTS

Michael Hayes	Catherine Parkes
Lori Fairbanks	Elaine Stanko
Lisa Boock	Lisa Willson
Vicki Gregory	Sue Carter
Kathy Bohr	Karen Neville
Sylvia Boggs	Colleen Drake
Barb from BSF	Judy Bush
Jana Smith	Sharon Pack
Michele Bruening	Janice Emerick
Joann from St. Mark's Bookstore	Derek
Cheryl BSF	Tammy BSF
Jan Loyd	Christine Holmes
Charlotte McGuire	David Hoskinson
Cindy Dooley	Candy Clark
Denise Dewitt	John Bruening

Many of these people listed wrote more than one license plate story. Some people's names are not listed, and a few wanted to remain anonymous.

I wish to acknowledge the contributions of the following special people:

Timothy Todd MD	Radosveta Stoyanov MD
Jack C. Lunderman Jr. MD	Elizabeth Hardy, PhD, Clinical Psychologist
Molly Hall MD	Jacqueline Countryman MD
Shirley Kleiman PT, DPT, OCS, cert. PSP	

I acknowledge the employees that worked with me at Redemption Press. Without their expertise this book would not have been possible. And most importantly to God to which all things are possible.

ORDER INFORMATION

REDEMPTION
P R E S S

To order additional copies of this book, please visit
www.redemption-press.com.
Also available at Christian bookstores, Amazon, and Barnes and Noble.

Printed in the USA
CPSIA information can be obtained
at www.ICGtesting.com
LVHW041656220324
775212LV00003B/651